bay books

contents

 easy *a little more care needed*  *more care needed*

American apple pie

When pilgrims first settled in North America, they took with them apple seeds and a love of pies, sowing a national love affair with this cherished homely dessert. Cooking apples yield the best results.

Preparation time **1 hour**
Total cooking time **1 hour**
Serves **4–6**

PASTRY
325 g (10¹/2 oz) plain flour
180 g (5³/4 oz) unsalted butter, cubed
2 tablespoons caster sugar

FILLING
800 g (1 lb 10 oz) large green apples
125 g (4 oz) sugar, and extra for sprinkling
1 teaspoon ground cinnamon
¹/4 teaspoon ground nutmeg
2¹/2 tablespoons plain flour
20 ml (³/4 fl oz) lemon juice
40 g (1¹/4 oz) unsalted butter, cubed

1 ` Preheat the oven to moderate 180°C (350°F/Gas 4). To make the pastry, work together the flour, butter, sugar and a pinch of salt in a food processor until the mixture resembles fine breadcrumbs. With the motor running, add 30 ml (1 fl oz) water and process until the mixture just comes together. Remove the dough, divide in half

and form each portion into a thick disc. Cover with plastic wrap and chill for 15–20 minutes.

2 To make the filling, peel, quarter and core the apples, then slice thinly and place in a large bowl. Combine the sugar, cinnamon, nutmeg, flour and a good pinch of salt, and sprinkle the mixture over the apple. Add the lemon juice and toss well.

3 On a lightly floured surface, roll out a pastry portion 2.5 mm (1/8 inch) thick, and 5 cm (2 inches) wider than a greased, shallow pie tin, 23 cm (9 inches) across the base. Carefully roll the dough onto a rolling pin, or fold into quarters, then ease into the tin. With your fingertips, press the dough into the tin to remove any air bubbles. Trim the excess pastry, leaving a 2.5 cm (1 inch) border of dough overhanging the edge of the tin.

4 Add the filling, then brush the pastry edges with water. Roll the remaining dough to the same thickness as before. Dot the apple with butter, place the dough on top and cut four steam holes. Trim the excess pastry, leaving a 1 cm (1/2 inch) overhang, then press the edges together to seal them. Crimp the edges by pinching the pastry between thumb and forefinger into a zigzag design. Brush the top with water and sprinkle with extra sugar, then bake for 55–60 minutes. Cool the pie on a rack, and serve warm or cold.

Crème brûlée

The literal translation of this rich dessert is 'burnt cream'. Just before serving, chilled custard is sprinkled with sugar, which is quickly caramelised under a grill to form a brittle topping, creating a delicious contrast in flavour and texture to the smooth, creamy custard beneath.

Preparation time **20 minutes + overnight refrigeration**
Total cooking time **55 minutes**
Serves 6

4 egg yolks
2 1/2 tablespoons caster sugar
300 ml (10 fl oz) thick (double) cream
300 ml (10 fl oz) cream
vanilla extract or essence
3 tablespoons sugar

1 Preheat the oven to slow 150°C (300°F/Gas 2). Have six 100 ml (3 1/4 fl oz) capacity ramekins ready.

2 Whisk the egg yolks and sugar in a large heatproof bowl. Set aside. Bring all the cream and a few drops of vanilla to the boil in a heavy-based pan, then reduce the heat and simmer for about 8 minutes. Remove the pan from the heat and slowly pour the cream onto the egg mixture, whisking vigorously so the eggs do not scramble. Strain the custard into a large jug, then pour into the ramekins.

3 Place the ramekins in a baking dish. Pour enough hot water into the dish to reach 1 cm (1/2 inch) below the ramekin rims. Bake the custard for 40–45 minutes, or until just firm to the touch. Remove from the oven, allow to cool, then cover and refrigerate overnight.

4 To make the caramel, evenly sprinkle some sugar over the top of each custard using a teaspoon. Without piercing the skin of the custard, spread the sugar out very gently using a finger or the spoon, then repeat to form a second layer of sugar. Remove any sugar from the inside edges of the ramekins as it will burn on the dish. Place the ramekins on a metal tray and glaze under a very hot grill for 2–3 minutes, or until the sugar has melted and is just beginning to give off a haze. Allow the glaze to set or harden before serving.

Chef's tips This wonderful dessert is enhanced by fruit. Before pouring the custard into the ramekins, arrange a few berries (strawberries or raspberries are ideal) in the bottom of the dish, or prunes presoaked in Armagnac.

For best results, use a blowtorch to brown the sugar on top of the custards.

Hot Cointreau and orange soufflé

A beautifully risen, hot soufflé is always a sight to behold. This spectacular dessert, flavoured simply with the sweetness of sun-drenched orange, will create a sensation among even the most discerning dinner guests.

Preparation time **35 minutes**
Total cooking time **20 minutes**
Serves **6**

softened butter, for greasing
110 g (3³/4 oz) caster sugar, and extra for lining
2 tablespoons orange juice
2 teaspoons grated orange rind
1 tablespoon Cointreau
250 ml (8 fl oz) milk
¹/2 vanilla pod, split lengthways
4 eggs, separated
1 tablespoon plain flour
1 tablespoon cornflour
sifted icing sugar, to dust

1 Preheat the oven to moderate 180°C (350°F/Gas 4). Brush the insides of six 8 x 4 cm (3 x 11/2 inch) soufflé dishes with softened butter, working the brush from the bottom upwards. Refrigerate to set and repeat.

2 Half-fill a soufflé dish with some sugar, and without placing your fingers inside the dish, rotate it so that a layer of sugar adheres to the butter. Tap out the excess sugar and repeat with the remaining soufflé dishes.

3 Place the orange juice and grated rind in a small pan over medium-high heat. Simmer for 3–5 minutes to reduce the volume by three quarters—the mixture should be quite syrupy. Pour in the Cointreau, scraping the base of the pan with a wooden spoon. Remove from the heat and allow to cool.

4 Bring the milk and vanilla pod slowly to the boil. In a bowl, and using a wooden spoon, mix together 75 g (21/2 oz) of the caster sugar and two of the egg yolks, then mix in the flour and cornflour. Remove the vanilla pod from the boiling milk; stir a little of the milk into the egg mixture, then add all the mixture to the milk in the pan. Beat rapidly with the wooden spoon over medium heat until the mixture thickens and comes to the boil. Boil gently for 1 minute to cook the flour, stirring continuously to prevent sticking.

5 Pour the mixture into a clean bowl, stir to cool it slightly, then beat in the reduced orange sauce. Stir in the remaining two egg yolks and run a small piece of butter over the surface to melt and prevent a skin forming. (If you prefer, place a sheet of baking paper on the surface instead.)

6 In a clean, dry bowl, whisk the egg whites until they form soft peaks. Add the remaining sugar and whisk for 30 seconds. Add a third of the egg whites to the milk mixture and lightly beat in until just combined. Using a large metal spoon, fold in the remaining egg whites gently but quickly. Do not overmix, as this will cause the mixture to lose volume and become heavy.

7 Set the soufflé dishes on a baking tray. Spoon in the mixture to completely fill each dish, smooth the surface of each soufflé and sprinkle with sifted icing sugar. Roll your thumb around the inside of each mould to create a ridge that will enable the soufflé to rise evenly (see Chef's techniques, page 63). Bake for 12 minutes, or until well risen with a light crust. The soufflés should feel just set when pressed lightly with a fingertip. Serve at once.

Chef's tip This soufflé—to the end of step 4—can be prepared a few hours in advance.

Fruit terrine

This luscious dessert yields a truly fruit-filled flavour with every tingling mouthful.
The secret is to use two loaf tins instead of one, sitting one on top of the other to
prevent the fruit floating to the top before the jelly has set.

Preparation time **40 minutes + 1–2 nights refrigeration**
Total cooking time **5–10 minutes**
Serves 8

100 g (3¹/4 oz) blackcurrants
120 g (4 oz) redcurrants
110 g (3³/4 oz) blueberries
350 g (11¹/4 oz) strawberries
225 g (7¹/4 oz) raspberries
4 leaves gelatine or 2 teaspoons gelatine powder
250 ml (8 fl oz) rosé wine
2 tablespoons caster sugar
1 tablespoon lemon juice
75 ml (2¹/2 fl oz) sieved raspberry purée
 (see Chef's tips)

1 Sort through all the fruit and remove any stalks, then gently mix the fruit together, taking care not to bruise or damage any. Soak the gelatine leaves or powder, following the Chef's techniques on page 63.
2 Carefully arrange the fruit into a 1 kg (2 lb) loaf tin measuring 13 x 23 x 7 cm (5 x 9 x 2³/4 inches), placing the smaller fruits on the bottom.

3 In a small pan, heat half the wine until it begins to simmer. Remove the pan from the heat and add the sugar, gelatine and lemon juice. Stir to dissolve. Add the remaining wine and the raspberry purée. Reserve 150 ml (5 fl oz) of the liquid and pour the rest over the fruit. Cover with plastic wrap. Place a lightly weighted 1 kg (2 lb) loaf tin on top, then refrigerate for at least 1 hour, or overnight if possible, until the terrine has set. Remove the top loaf tin and plastic wrap.
4 Gently warm the reserved wine-liquid and pour over the surface of the terrine. Cover again with plastic wrap and refrigerate overnight to set.
5 Just before serving, turn out the terrine by dipping the base of the tin very briefly in hot water and inverting it onto a plate. Slice the terrine, decorate with some extra fresh berries, and serve with crème fraîche.

Chef's tips Sieving 150 g (5 oz) of raspberries will produce the required quantity of raspberry purée.

Do not rinse the raspberries, and only rinse the other fruit if it is sandy.

Small strawberries give the best results in this fruit terrine, but if they are not available, you could use larger strawberries, cut in half.

Pink grapefruit sorbet

This sublime sorbet may be served in a tall glass as a refreshing dessert, or in a sherry glass as a palate cleanser. For best results, use an ice-cream churn.

*Preparation time **30 minutes + churning or beating + freezing***
*Total cooking time **1 minute***
Serves 6

175 g (5³/4 oz) caster sugar
200 ml (6¹/2 fl oz) pink or yellow grapefruit juice (about 3 grapefruit)
80 ml (2³/4 fl oz) lemon juice
250 ml (8 fl oz) dry white wine
75 ml (2¹/2 fl oz) Campari
6 sprigs of lemon balm or mint, to garnish

1 Stir the sugar and 175 ml (5³/4 fl oz) water in a small pan over low heat until the sugar dissolves. Bring to the boil, and allow to boil for 1 minute. Remove from the heat and leave to cool.

2 Combine the grapefruit and lemon juice and strain into a jug. Add the wine, Campari and cooled syrup.

3 Churn in an ice-cream maker for 30–40 minutes, or until thick and slushy, then transfer to a stainless steel container. Cover well with plastic wrap, then foil, and freeze for 1 hour before use.

4 Alternatively, freeze the mixture in a stainless steel container for about 3 hours, or until firm. Scoop into a large bowl and beat with an electric beater for 1–2 minutes, or until thick and creamy. Return the mixture to the container and freeze for 3 hours. Repeat the beating and freezing twice, then freeze overnight.

5 Remove from the freezer and refrigerate for about 20 minutes before serving. Scoop the mixture into well-chilled glasses and decorate each with a sprig of lemon balm or mint.

Chef's tip This sorbet can be frozen for up to 3 months.

Twice-baked chocolate cakes

These dark, fudgy cakes are sinfully rich and totally irresistible, with a dense base and a soufflé-like top that rises beautifully with the help of a paper collar. Sheer indulgence!

Preparation time *1 hour 25 minutes*
Total cooking time *35 minutes*
Serves 6

180 g (5³/4 oz) dark chocolate
150 g (5 oz) unsalted butter
3 tablespoons cocoa powder
6 eggs, separated
120 g (4 oz) caster sugar
cocoa and icing sugar, to dust

1 Preheat the oven to warm 170°C (325°F/Gas 3). Lightly grease six baking rings, each 7–8 cm (3 inches) across and 2 cm (3/4 inch) tall. (You can use 12 egg rings instead, stacking them two-high to form six 'rings'.) Line a baking tray with baking paper, grease the paper and set the baking rings on the tray.
2 Cut six strips of baking paper, each one 30 x 11 cm (12 x 41/2 inches) long. Make a 1 cm (1/2 inch) fold along one long edge of each strip, then carefully make 1 cm (1/2 inch) diagonal cuts into the fold, spaced about 5 mm (1/4 inch) apart. Line the rings with the strips of paper so that the diagonal cuts sit very flat on the base of the tray. Press out any air bubbles with a pastry brush and refrigerate until ready to fill.

3 Melt the chocolate in a heatproof bowl set over a pan of simmering water. Add the butter and cocoa powder, whisk until smooth, and set aside.
4 Whisk the egg whites in a clean, dry bowl until stiff peaks form, then gradually beat in half the sugar until smooth and glossy. In a separate bowl, beat together the egg yolks and the remaining caster sugar for 5 minutes, or until light in colour and a ribbon forms when the whisk is lifted out of the bowl. Gently fold in the egg whites using a rubber spatula or large metal spoon. Gently fold in the chocolate mixture.
5 Divide half the mixture evenly between the rings, being careful not to get batter on the paper above. Bake for 15 minutes, then remove and cool completely. (The cakes will collapse and flatten.) Spoon the remaining mixture into each ring, covering the cake. Bake for 15–20 minutes. When cooked, the centre of the top of the cakes will stay steady when the tray is gently jiggled.
6 Slide a thin metal spatula under each ring and carefully loosen the cakes from the baking tray. Remove the rings, carefully peel the paper sleeves from the cakes and place on a serving plate. Dust with a little combined cocoa and icing sugar and serve at once.

Chef's tip Filling the rings with cake mixture is most easily done using a piping bag fitted with a medium tip.

Thin apple tart

This spectacular tart—Tarte fine aux pommes—has a crisp shortcrust base spread with almond cream and topped with glazed apples. This recipe calls for Golden Delicious apples, but whichever variety you use, recall the ancient wisdom of Horace: the best apples of all are those picked by the light of a waning moon!

*Preparation time **1 hour + 40 minutes refrigeration***
*Total cooking time **1 hour***
*Serves **6–8***

SHORTCRUST PASTRY
100 g (3¹/4 oz) plain flour
50 g (1³/4 oz) icing sugar
50 g (1³/4 oz) unsalted butter
I egg yolk
vanilla extract or essence

ALMOND CREAM
3 tablespoons icing sugar
30 g (I oz) unsalted butter, softened
I teaspoon vanilla extract or essence
I egg yolk
3 tablespoons ground almonds

500 g (I lb) Golden Delicious apples, or similar variety
juice of I lemon
apricot jam, for glazing

1 To make the pastry, sift the flour and icing sugar into a bowl, then rub in the butter until the mixture resembles breadcrumbs. Make a well in the centre and add the egg yolk, a few drops of vanilla, a pinch of salt and enough cold water to help form a dough. Turn out onto a floured surface and gather the dough together to make a smooth ball. Cover with plastic wrap and refrigerate for 30 minutes, or until just firm.

2 Preheat the oven to moderate 180°C (350°F/Gas 4). Remove the plastic wrap from the chilled pastry, then very gently roll out the pastry between two sheets of greaseproof or baking paper to a thickness of 2.5 mm (¹/8 inch). Carefully ease the pastry into a greased, shallow loose-bottomed flan tin, 22 cm (8³/4 inches) across the base.

3 Blind bake the pastry for 20 minutes, following the Chef's techniques on page 62. Remove the rice or baking beans and baking paper, then bake for a further 10 minutes, covering the pastry with foil if the pastry looks as though it might burn. Remove from the oven and allow to cool.

4 To make the almond cream, beat together the icing sugar, butter and vanilla until light and creamy. Add the egg yolk and beat well, then add the ground almonds. Spread the mixture in an even layer over the cooled pastry shell.

5 Peel, quarter and core the apples, then sprinkle them with lemon juice. Thinly slice the apples and arrange in overlapping circles over the layer of almond cream. Bake for 20–25 minutes, or until the apples are cooked. Set on a wire rack to cool.

6 When the tart has cooled, place some apricot jam in a small pan and bring to the boil. (Add a spoonful of water if the jam becomes too thick for spreading.) Sieve the jam and, using a pastry brush, lightly dab the surface of the tart with the jam—this will give the apples a nice shine and prevent them drying out.

Chef's tips Handle the pastry as little as possible, and work quickly and lightly.

Make sure the tart has cooled before brushing it with jam. If the tart is still hot, the fruit will simply soak up the jam and the tart will lose its shine when it cools.

Vanilla ice cream

No commercial ice cream can ever compare with the creamy, decadent richness of the home-made variety. This classic favourite is peppered with fine black specks: the tiny seeds of the vanilla pod, which release a fabulous flavour. For a light, smooth result every time, with minimal fuss, an ice-cream churn is highly recommended.

*Preparation time **20 minutes + churning or beating + freezing***
*Total cooking time **10 minutes***
Serves 4

5 egg yolks
100 g (3¹/4 oz) caster sugar
375 ml (12 fl oz) milk
1 vanilla pod, split lengthways
125 ml (4 fl oz) thick (double) cream

1 Whisk the egg yolks and sugar in a heatproof bowl until thick and creamy and almost white. Bring the milk and vanilla pod slowly to the boil in a heavy-based pan. Gradually whisk the boiling milk into the eggs and sugar, then transfer the mixture to a clean pan. Stir constantly with a wooden spoon over low heat for about 3–5 minutes, or until the custard thickly coats the back of the spoon. Ensure that the mixture does not boil, as this will cause it to separate.

2 Pour through a fine strainer into a clean bowl. Place the bowl in some iced water to cool. When the custard is very cold, stir in the cream, then pour the mixture into an ice-cream churn and churn for 10–20 minutes, or until the paddle leaves a trail in the ice cream, or the ice cream holds its own shape. Remove from the churn and freeze in an airtight, stainless steel container for 3–4 hours or overnight.

3 Alternatively, freeze the custard and cream mixture in a 1 litre container for 3 hours, or until firm. Scoop into a large bowl and beat with an electric beater for 1–2 minutes, or until thick and creamy. Return the mixture to the container and freeze for 3 hours. Repeat the beating and freezing twice, then freeze overnight.

Chef's tip This ice cream can take on a range of flavours. A little coffee extract may be added to the custard at the end of step 1, or 50–100 g (1³/4–3¹/4 oz) chopped chocolate may be added to the milk before boiling. Another delicious option is to fold amaretto or crushed biscuits into the frozen ice cream before it is stored.

Thin shortbreads with fresh cream and fruit

*This easy-to-assemble dessert is a wicked union of sweet red fruit and luscious whipped cream,
anchored in rounds of lemon-tinged shortbread.*

Preparation time 45 minutes + refrigeration
Total cooking time 20–25 minutes
Serves 4–6

SHORTBREAD PASTRY
300 g (10 oz) unsalted butter, softened
150 g (5 oz) icing sugar
finely grated rind of 1 lemon
vanilla extract or essence
1 egg, lightly beaten
450 g (14¹/4 oz) plain flour, sifted

FILLING
200 ml (6¹/2 fl oz) thick (double) cream
1 teaspoon vanilla extract or essence
caster sugar, to taste
400 g (12³/4 oz) assorted red fruits, such as
*   strawberries, raspberries and redcurrants*

40 g (1¹/4 oz) icing sugar, for dusting
fresh mint leaves, to garnish

1 Brush two baking trays with melted butter and refrigerate. Preheat the oven to warm 160°C (315°F/ Gas 2–3). To make the pastry, cream the butter and sugar until pale and smooth. Stir in the rind and a few drops of vanilla. Add the egg gradually, beating well after each addition. Add the flour in one batch and stir until combined: the mixture will be very soft and sticky.

2 Divide the mixture in two. Roll out each portion 2.5 mm (1/8 inch) thick between two layers of well-floured greaseproof or baking paper, working quickly and lightly. Place on the chilled trays with the paper still attached, then refrigerate until firm.

3 Slide the pastry off the trays onto a work surface. Remove the top piece of paper, dip an 8.5 cm (3¹/2 inch) fluted pastry-cutter in flour and cut three discs per serve. Ease the discs off the bottom sheet of paper onto the buttered baking trays and prick with a fork. Bake for 20–25 minutes, or until golden; allow to cool briefly before removing from the tray to cool on a rack.

4 To make the filling, pour the cream into a bowl, add the vanilla, and sugar to taste. Whisk into soft peaks. (Do not overwhisk as the cream will overthicken and split.) Spoon into a piping bag fitted with an 8-cut star nozzle.

5 To assemble, pipe some cream onto the middle of a disc; arrange some fruit around the cream (but not over the edge). Top with a disc, repeat the fruit and cream, then top with a third disc, dusted with icing sugar. Finish the remaining rounds, reserving some fruit. Transfer to serving plates and decorate with mint and reserved fruit.

Chocolate and Cointreau mousse

Mousse in French literally means froth or foam. This melt-in-the-mouth mousse marries the classic flavours of chocolate and orange, is simple to prepare, and makes a magical finale to any meal.

*Preparation time **40 minutes + 1 hour refrigeration***
*Total cooking time **5 minutes***
Serves 4–6

125 g (4 oz) dark chocolate
50 g (1³/4 oz) unsalted butter
70 ml (2¹/4 fl oz) orange juice
2¹/2 tablespoons cocoa powder
2 eggs, separated
25 ml (³/4 fl oz) Cointreau
100 ml (3¹/4 fl oz) cream, for whipping
1 egg white, extra
1¹/2 tablespoons caster sugar
orange segments and whipped cream, to serve

1 Place the chocolate, butter and orange juice in a heatproof bowl over a pan of just-simmering water. When the chocolate and butter have melted, stir in the cocoa powder. Remove from the heat and whisk in the egg yolks and Cointreau. Leave to cool.
2 In a chilled bowl, beat the cream until soft peaks form. Cover and refrigerate until ready to use.
3 Beat all the egg whites in a clean, dry bowl until soft peaks form. Add the sugar; beat until smooth and glossy.
4 Using a large metal spoon, gently fold the egg whites into the cooled chocolate mixture. Before they are completely incorporated, fold in the whipped cream. Transfer the mixture into individual serving dishes or a large serving bowl and refrigerate for at least 1 hour. Serve with orange segments and whipped cream.

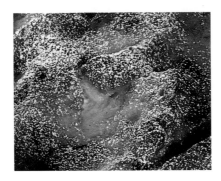

Bread and butter pudding with panettone

When the yearning strikes for a homely dessert, bread and butter pudding is hard to beat.
For special occasions, this humble and economical dish can be transformed into something really
marvellous with glacé fruits, a dash of rum, some brioche or, as in this case, Italian panettone.

*Preparation time **20 minutes***
*Total cooking time **50 minutes***
Serves 4

3 tablespoons sultanas
2 tablespoons rum, brandy or amaretto
250 g (8 oz) panettone
3 eggs
3 tablespoons caster sugar
500 ml (16 fl oz) milk
1 vanilla pod, split lengthways
1 tablespoon apricot jam, warmed
icing sugar, to dust

1 Preheat the oven to warm 160°C (315°F/Gas 2–3). Place the sultanas in a 23 cm (9 inch) oval pie dish and pour the alcohol over the top.
2 Cut the panettone to make two or three round slices about 1 cm (1/2 inch) thick, then remove the crust. Cut each slice into four quarters (almost triangles). Neatly overlap them in the base of the pie dish.
3 Whisk the eggs and sugar in a heatproof bowl until just combined. Place the milk and vanilla pod in a pan, bring to the boil, then slowly pour the scalding milk into the egg and sugar mixture, whisking continuously.
4 Pour the mixture through a fine strainer into the pie dish, over the panettone. Place the pie dish in a baking tray half full of hot water. Cook for 40–45 minutes, or until the custard has set and is golden brown.
5 Remove the pie dish from the oven and, while the pudding is still warm, brush the surface with the warm apricot jam. Sprinkle with icing sugar and serve either hot or cold.

Chef's tips If the panettone is not a sweet one, simply increase the sugar to taste.
  Fruit loaf is a perfect alternative to panettone as it already has a loaf shape. Simply cut off the crusts, slice the bread and cut each slice in half to form triangles.

Spiced poached pears with orange butter

In this simply elegant dessert, the pears are gently infused with the flavours of real vanilla and star anise, then fringed with wisps of candied peel, and served with a Cointreau-laced orange sauce.

*Preparation time **1 hour***
*Total cooking time **1 hour***
Serves 4

1 lemon
800 g (1 lb 10 oz) oranges
660 g (1 lb 6 oz) sugar
1 vanilla pod, split lengthways
3 sticks cinnamon
10 whole black peppercorns
4 star anise
3 cloves
pinch of nutmeg
6 pears, about 1.5 kg (3 lb)
fresh mint leaves, to garnish

ORANGE BUTTER
400 ml (12³/4 fl oz) orange juice
120 g (4 oz) unsalted butter, cut into cubes
2 tablespoons Cointreau

1 Peel the rind off the lemon and an orange with a vegetable peeler, without scraping the bitter white pith. Place the rind in a large pan with 2 litres water and 500 g (1 lb) of the sugar. Wrap the whole spices in muslin for easy removal later, and add them to the pan with the nutmeg. Stir over a low heat until the sugar has dissolved, then bring to a gentle simmer.

2 Peel the pears, leaving the stems intact, and add them to the simmering liquid. Allow them to simmer gently for 20 minutes, or until easily pierced with a knife tip. They should be just tender, but not soft. Remove from the heat and allow to cool in the liquid.

3 To make the orange butter, bring the orange juice to the boil in a small pan, then reduce the heat and simmer for 30 minutes, or until reduced by three quarters. Remove from the heat and whisk in the butter, a few pieces at a time. Whisk in the Cointreau and set aside.

4 Peel the rind from the remaining oranges, avoiding the bitter white pith. Cut the rind into thin strips and set aside. Cut the tops and bottoms off the oranges and discard. Place the oranges on a cutting board and with a sharp knife, cut from top to bottom, following the curve of the fruit to expose the flesh. Cut between the membranes to remove the orange segments. Set aside.

5 Place the strips of orange rind in a small pan and cover with water. Bring to the boil, strain the rind and rinse with cold water. Return to the pan with 160 ml (2³/4 fl oz) water and the remaining sugar. Stir over low heat to dissolve the sugar, then bring to the boil. Reduce the heat and leave the rinds to slowly candy in the syrup for 20 minutes—they will become translucent. Strain over a bowl, reserving the liquid. Add the liquid to the orange butter, and cool the rinds on a piece of baking paper.

6 Remove two of the cooled pears and cut them in half. Remove the cores and stems, then slice the pear halves thinly. Place a sliced half on each plate, as well as a whole pear. Drizzle the orange butter around and arrange some candied rind on top of the pear slices. Decorate with the orange segments and fresh mint.

Chef's tip Poached pears will improve in flavour and texture if prepared 1 or 2 days in advance. They can be refrigerated for up to 1 week in the syrup. For extra colour, add 2 tablespoons of grenadine syrup to the sugar mixture when candying the orange rind.

Hot passion fruit soufflés

Feather-light, these wonderful soufflés tantalise the tastebuds with the tart sweetness and tropical perfume of passion fruit.

Preparation time **20 minutes**
Total cooking time **20 minutes**
Serves 4

softened unsalted butter, for greasing
120 g (4 oz) caster sugar, and extra for coating
12 passion fruit or 120 g (4 oz) passion fruit pulp
6 egg whites
icing sugar, for dusting

1 Prepare four 10 cm (4 inch) 250 ml (8 fl oz) capacity ramekins or individual soufflé moulds by brushing the inside of each with softened butter, using a pastry brush. Refrigerate the moulds until the butter is firm, then brush on another layer of butter and chill again. Half-fill one of the moulds with the extra sugar, and without placing your fingers inside the mould, rotate it so that a layer of sugar adheres to the butter. Tap out the excess sugar and use it to coat the other moulds.

2 Preheat the oven to warm 160°C (315°F/Gas 2–3). Pass the passion fruit pulp through a sieve into a bowl and add 60 g (2 oz) sugar. Discard the seeds.

3 Whisk the egg whites until soft peaks form. Sprinkle the remaining sugar onto the egg whites and whisk for 1 minute. Gently fold the egg whites into the passion fruit pulp. Spoon a quarter of the mixture into each mould and smooth the surface. Sprinkle the top of each soufflé with sifted icing sugar, then run your thumb around the inside of the mould to create a ridge to help the soufflé rise evenly (see Chef's techniques, page 63).

4 Place the moulds in a baking tray or large ovenproof dish, and pour in enough hot water to reach halfway up the moulds. Bake for 20 minutes, or until well risen. Once cooked, remove from the oven, sprinkle with more sifted icing sugar and serve immediately.

Bavarian vanilla cream

A bavarois is an egg-based custard folded through with whipped cream, and flavoured with chocolate, coffee, praline or even fruit. This bavarois is simply laced with real vanilla.

Preparation time *1 hour + 1 hour refrigeration*
Total cooking time *10 minutes*
Serves 4

3 leaves gelatine or 1 1/2 teaspoons gelatine powder

2 eggs, separated

3 tablespoons caster sugar

250 ml (8 fl oz) milk

1 vanilla pod, split lengthways

125 ml (4 fl oz) thick (double) cream, lightly whipped

1 Lightly grease four 250 ml (8 fl oz) capacity moulds of any shape, then soak the gelatine leaves or powder, following the Chef's techniques on page 63.

2 Beat the egg yolks and sugar in a bowl until thick, creamy and almost white. Slowly bring the milk and vanilla pod to the boil.

3 Follow the method for making custard in the Chef's techniques on page 63. Stir the soaked gelatine into the hot custard, ensuring the gelatine dissolves completely, strain into a clean bowl, then leave over a bowl of ice until almost at the point of setting, stirring occasionally, and checking often.

4 Whisk the egg whites until stiff—they should stand in shiny peaks when the whisk is lifted. Using a metal spoon, fold the lightly whipped cream into the cold custard, then carefully fold in the egg whites.

5 Spoon the mixture into the moulds and refrigerate for at least 1 hour, or until set. Unmould by gently shaking at an angle of 45°, or dipping the base of the mould briefly in boiling water and tapping onto a serving dish.

Chef's tips The egg whites should not be whisked too far in advance: standing will make the volume drop, and also result in a dry, granular texture. Adding a pinch of sugar while the egg whites are lightly foaming will stabilise them and help them whisk stiff more easily.

Ensure the custard is cold before adding the cream: if the cream melts, the dessert will lose volume.

Rhubarb and almond tart

This tart has a rich, moist filling and can be enjoyed on its own, or with crème anglaise or ice cream. It keeps well and can be made a few days in advance. Fresh plums, apricots or pears can be used instead of rhubarb.

Preparation time **1 hour + 40 minutes refrigeration**
Total cooking time **40 minutes**
Serves 6–8

PASTRY
125 g (4 oz) unsalted butter, softened
3 tablespoons caster sugar
I egg, beaten
200 g (6 1/2 oz) plain flour

ALMOND CREAM
100 g (3 1/4 oz) unsalted butter, softened
100 g (3 1/4 oz) caster sugar
2 teaspoons finely grated lemon rind
2 eggs
100 g (3 1/4 oz) ground almonds
I tablespoon plain flour

2 tablespoons raspberry jam
I stick rhubarb, thinly sliced
2 tablespoons flaked almonds
2 tablespoons apricot jam
icing sugar, for dusting

1 To make the pastry, beat the butter and sugar in a bowl until well blended using a wooden spoon or electric beaters. Add the egg gradually, beating well after each addition. Sift in the flour and a pinch of salt and mix lightly using a flat-bladed knife until the mixture just comes together—do not overmix. Gather together to form a rough ball and place on a large piece of plastic wrap. Gently flatten to a 1 cm (1/2 inch) thickness, then wrap and refrigerate for 20 minutes.

2 To make the almond cream, beat the butter, sugar and lemon rind in a small bowl using a wooden spoon, whisk or electric beaters. Gradually beat in the eggs. Stir in the almonds and flour and set aside.

3 To assemble, roll out the pastry on a floured surface (or between two sheets of baking paper) 2.5 mm (1/8 inch) thick. Ease into a greased, loose-bottomed, fluted or plain flan tin, 20 cm (8 inches) across the base. Trim the edges, pierce the base lightly with a fork and spread with raspberry jam. Spread the almond cream over the top, just level with the pastry edge. Decorate with rhubarb, slightly pushing into the almond cream. Sprinkle with flaked almonds and chill for 20 minutes.

4 Preheat the oven to moderate 180°C (350°F/Gas 4). Place the tart on a baking tray and bake for 10 minutes to help set the pastry. Reduce the oven temperature to warm 160°C (315°F/Gas 2–3) and bake for a further 30–35 minutes, or until the almond filling is golden brown and springs back when lightly touched.

5 In a small pan, heat the apricot jam with 3 teaspoons water. When the mixture has melted and begins to boil, sieve it into a small bowl, and while still hot, brush it over the tart. Allow the jam to cool, then sift a light dusting of icing sugar across the top.

Chef's tips Handle the pastry as little as possible: work quickly and lightly. Always rest or chill pastry before rolling to make it easier to manage. Resting just before baking helps prevent shrinkage and loss of shape.

To make the pastry in a food processor, process the flour, butter and sugar into fine crumbs, add the egg and process in short bursts until the pastry just comes together. Tip onto a lightly floured work surface and draw the pastry together by hand.

Creamed rice pudding

Whipped cream makes this rice pudding extravagantly rich and creamy.
A sharp fruit sauce or compote is the perfect accompaniment.

*Preparation time **10 minutes***
*Total cooking time **30 minutes***
Serves 4–6

3 tablespoons short-grain rice
600 ml (20 fl oz) milk
1 vanilla pod, split lengthways
2 tablespoons caster sugar
150 ml (5 fl oz) cream, for whipping

1 Place the rice in a colander and rinse thoroughly under running water until the water runs clear. Drain.
2 Pour the milk into a medium heavy-based pan, add the vanilla pod and rice, then bring slowly to the boil.

Reduce the heat and gently simmer, stirring often, for about 30 minutes, or until the rice is soft and creamy. When a spoon is drawn across the base of the pan, a clear parting in the rice should be left behind.
3 Stir in the sugar and transfer the mixture to a large bowl. Remove the vanilla pod, cover the surface with plastic wrap and allow to cool. Lightly whip the cream in a separate bowl until soft peaks form. When the pudding is cold, carefully fold in the cream. Serve with a fruit sauce or compote.

Chef's tip Because this dessert is so rich, you may choose to add only half of the whipped cream. To vary the flavour, try adding a small pinch of cinnamon or nutmeg with the sugar.

Apple strudel

In Vienna it is said that in the making of a perfect apple strudel, the dough is stretched so finely that a love letter may be read through it.

Preparation time **40 minutes + 30 minutes resting**
Total cooking time **50 minutes**
Serves **6–8**

185 g (6 oz) strong or plain flour
1 egg, lightly beaten
120 g (4 oz) unsalted butter
90 g (3 oz) fresh breadcrumbs
3 tablespoons caster sugar
2 teaspoons ground cinnamon
600 g (1 1/4 lb) cooking or very sharp dessert apples
60 g (2 oz) sultanas
icing sugar, for dusting

1 Sift the flour and a pinch of salt into a large bowl. Make a well in the centre, add the beaten egg and 75 ml (2 1/2 fl oz) warm water, and mix with your hands to a smooth dough. With the bowl tipped to one side, and with open fingers, beat the dough, rotating your wrist. The dough is ready when it pulls away from the bowl and is difficult to beat. Place in a clean, lightly floured bowl, cover and leave in a warm place for 15 minutes.

2 Melt half of the butter in a pan. Slowly fry the breadcrumbs until golden brown, then set aside to cool in a bowl. Mix the sugar and cinnamon in a small bowl. Preheat the oven to moderate 180°C (350°F/Gas 4).

3 Thoroughly flour one side of a large clean tea towel, place the pastry on top and, with your fingers, gently stretch the dough to a large rectangle about 50 x 60 cm (20 x 24 inches); cover with a tea towel and set aside for 15 minutes. Melt the remaining butter and set aside.

4 Peel, quarter, core and finely slice the apples, and combine with the breadcrumbs, cinnamon mixture and sultanas. Brush the dough liberally with the melted butter, then sprinkle the apple mixture all over the dough. Trim away the thick edge with a pair of scissors.

5 Pick up the tea towel from the shorter side, and push away and down from you to lightly roll the strudel up like a swiss roll. Tip the strudel carefully onto a tray, seam-side down or to one side. Leave the strudel straight, or curve it lightly into the traditional 'crescent'. Brush the pastry well with any remaining butter.

6 Bake for 35–45 minutes, or until crisp and golden. Cool slightly, sprinkle with icing sugar and serve warm with vanilla custard, ice cream or whipped cream.

Clafoutis

This classic dessert is based on a dish originating in the French country region of Limousin, where clafoutis is enjoyed when sweet, dark cherries are ripe. Cherries are the favoured fruit for this dessert, although plums or pears may also be used.

Preparation time **40 minutes**
Total cooking time **45 minutes**
Serves 4

1 fresh peach or 2 tinned peach halves, drained of syrup
250 g (8 oz) cherries
500 ml (16 fl oz) thick (double) cream
1 vanilla pod, split lengthways
6 egg yolks
1 egg
1 tablespoon custard powder
2¹/2 tablespoons plain flour
25 ml (³/4 fl oz) Cointreau
icing sugar, for dusting

1 Preheat the oven to slow 150°C (300°F/Gas 2). If you are using a fresh peach, plunge it in boiling water for 10–20 seconds, then transfer to a bowl of iced water. Peel the peach and cut around the fruit towards the stone. Gently twist the halves in opposite directions to expose the stone, then lift out the stone with a knife. If the peach is too slippery, simply cut the flesh from the stone. Process or sieve one peach half and measure out 50 ml (1³/4 fl oz) of purée. Slice the remaining peach half into neat segments and set aside. Pit the cherries and set aside.

2 Place the cream in a heavy-based pan with the vanilla pod, then heat until scalding—this is when bubbles form around the edge of the cream surface, yet the cream is not boiling. Remove the vanilla pod.

3 Whisk the egg yolks and the whole egg together in a large bowl. Beat in the custard powder and flour, then stir in the peach purée. Whisk the scalding cream into the egg mixture. Add the Cointreau and stir.

4 Lightly grease a 2 litre capacity shallow ovenproof dish with softened butter. Place all the fruit in the dish. Pour the custard over and bake for about 40 minutes, or until a skewer inserted into the centre of the dessert comes out clean. Immediately sift the icing sugar over the top. Serve hot.

Iced raspberry soufflé

*This chilled raspberry soufflé always looks wonderful and is a great
conversation piece. It can also be made days—if not weeks—ahead,
leaving more time for you to spend with your guests.*

*Preparation time **45 minutes + 6 hours freezing
+ 30 minutes standing***
*Total cooking time **10 minutes***
*Serves **4–6***

550 g (1 lb 1³/4 oz) raspberries
250 g (8 oz) caster sugar
5 egg whites
400 ml (12³/4 fl oz) cream, for whipping
200 ml (6¹/2 fl oz) cream, for whipping, extra
fresh raspberries, to garnish
sprigs of fresh mint, to garnish

1 Purée the raspberries in a food processor, then press
through a fine sieve to eliminate the seeds. Weigh out
300 g (10 oz) of raspberry purée and set aside.
2 Cut out a piece of greaseproof or baking paper
to measure 25 x 9 cm (10 x 3¹/2 inches). Wrap the
paper around the outside of a 1 litre, 18 cm (7 inch)
soufflé dish to make a collar. Secure the overlapping

paper in place with tape or kitchen string, keeping the
paper free of creases.
3 Place the caster sugar and 60 ml (2 fl oz) water in a
medium heavy-based pan and heat gently to dissolve
the sugar. Bring the syrup to the boil, then follow the
Chef's techniques for making Italian meringue on
page 63.
4 In a separate bowl, whip the first quantity of cream
to soft peaks.
5 Using a metal spoon, gently fold the meringue into
the reserved raspberry purée until thoroughly mixed,
then fold in the cream until the streaks disappear. Be
careful not to overmix, as this will cause the cream to
thicken and separate and make the soufflé look grainy.
6 Spoon the mixture into the soufflé dish right up to
the edge of the paper collar, then gently smooth the
surface of the soufflé. Freeze for a minimum of 6 hours.
Just before serving, peel off the paper collar and allow
the soufflé to stand for 30 minutes to soften. Whip the
extra cream and use it to decorate the soufflé. Top with
the fresh raspberries and sprigs of mint.

Lemon meringue pie

This time-honoured favourite—a shortcrust pastry case smothered by a creamy lemon filling and a layer of meringue—is often served for Sunday lunch. It should be baked and served on the same day.

*Preparation time **45 minutes + 40 minutes refrigeration***
*Total cooking time **45 minutes***
*Serves **6***

SHORTCRUST PASTRY
200 g (6¹/2 oz) plain flour, sifted
1 teaspoon caster sugar
100 g (3¹/4 oz) unsalted butter, chopped
1 egg
1 teaspoon vanilla extract or essence

LEMON FILLING
3 egg yolks
150 g (5 oz) caster sugar
2 teaspoons finely grated lemon rind
juice of 3 lemons
30 g (1 oz) unsalted butter

200 g (6¹/2 oz) caster sugar
4 egg whites
1 tablespoon icing sugar, for dusting

1 To make the shortcrust pastry, sieve the flour, sugar and a good pinch of salt into a bowl. Add the butter and rub between your fingertips until the mixture resembles fine breadcrumbs. Make a well in the centre. Combine the egg, vanilla and 2 teaspoons water and pour into the well. Slowly stir together with a flat-bladed knife, adding more flour if the mixture is slightly sticky. Gather the dough together in a ball, wrap in plastic wrap and refrigerate for 20 minutes.

2 Preheat the oven to moderate 180°C (350°F/Gas 4). Gently roll the pastry between two sheets of baking paper to about 2.5 mm (¹/8 inch) thick, then ease into a lightly greased, loose-bottomed fluted flan tin, 22 cm (8³/4 inches) across the base. Blind bake for 10 minutes, following the Chef's techniques on page 62. Remove the rice or baking beans and the paper. Bake for 10 more minutes, or until the centre begins to colour. Remove from the oven and cool on a wire rack.

3 To prepare the filling, heat a medium pan of water until gently simmering. Whisk or beat the egg yolks and sugar in a large heatproof bowl until light and creamy. Add the lemon rind, juice and then the butter. Sit the bowl over the pan of barely simmering water and whisk continuously for 15–20 minutes, or until thickened. When ready, the mixture will leave a 'ribbon' when drizzled from the whisk. While the filling is still hot, pour into the cool, prebaked flan case.

4 Place the sugar and 50 ml (1³/4 fl oz) water in a medium heavy-based pan and heat gently to dissolve the sugar. Bring to the boil, then follow the Chef's techniques for making Italian meringue on page 63.

5 Place the meringue in a piping bag fitted with a 1 cm (¹/2 inch) star nozzle. Starting in the centre, pipe the meringue in continuous concentric circles covering the entire flan, keeping the meringue inside the pastry edge. Dust the surface with icing sugar. Bake for 5 minutes, or until the meringue is lightly coloured. Leave to cool and then refrigerate for 20 minutes, or until the filling is set.

Chef's tip If possible, refrigerate the dough overnight. This helps prevent the pastry shrinking during cooking.

Crêpes Suzette

*In this illustrious dessert, very fine pancakes are warmed in a lightly caramelised
orange butter sauce, then doused with Cointreau and ignited to flaming glory,
ending any repast on a note of unforgettable flourish.*

Preparation time **30 minutes + 30 minutes resting**
Total cooking time **45 minutes**
Makes 12 crêpes

CREPE BATTER
90 g (3 oz) plain flour
1 teaspoon caster sugar
2 eggs, plus 1 egg yolk, lightly beaten
170 ml (5 1/2 fl oz) milk
25 g (3/4 oz) clarified butter, melted (see page 62)

clarified butter, for cooking (see page 62)

SAUCE
4 white sugar cubes
800 g (1 lb 10 oz) oranges
40 g (1 1/4 oz) clarified butter, melted (see page 62)
3 tablespoons caster sugar
45 ml (1 1/2 fl oz) Cointreau
30 ml (1 fl oz) brandy

1 To make the batter, sift the flour into a bowl with a pinch of salt and the sugar. Make a well in the centre, then add the eggs and extra egg yolk. Mix well with a wooden spoon or whisk, gradually incorporating the flour. Combine the milk with 60 ml (2 fl oz) water and gradually add to the batter. Add the clarified butter and beat until smooth. Cover and set aside for 30 minutes.
2 Melt a little clarified butter in a shallow heavy-based or non-stick pan measuring 15–17 cm (6–6 3/4 inches) across the base. When a haze forms, pour off any surplus butter, leaving a fine coating sufficient to cook one crêpe. Tilt the pan and pour in a little batter, swirling to coat just the bottom of the pan with a thin layer. Cook for 1–2 minutes, or until the edges are lightly brown. Loosen the edges with a flat-bladed knife or spatula and turn or flip the crêpe over. Cook for about 1 minute, then turn onto a sheet of greaseproof or baking paper and cover with a tea towel. Repeat until all the batter has been used up, each time lightly coating the pan with clarified butter.
3 To make the sauce, rub all the sugar cube sides over the rind of an orange to soak up the oily zest, then crush the cubes with the back of a wooden spoon. Juice the oranges to produce 315 ml (10 fl oz) liquid. Over gentle heat, melt the clarified butter in a wide shallow pan or frying pan. Dissolve the crushed sugar in the butter, then add the caster sugar. Cook, stirring, for 2 minutes. Slowly add the orange juice, keeping well clear of the pan as the mixture may spit. Increase the heat to medium and simmer until reduced by one third.
4 Fold the crêpes in half, then into triangles. Place them in the orange sauce, slightly overlapping, with their points showing. Tilt the pan, scoop up the sauce and pour it over the crêpes to moisten them well.
5 Cook over low heat for 2 minutes. Turn off the heat and have a saucepan lid ready in case you need to put out the flame. Pour the Cointreau and brandy over the sauce without stirring. Immediately light the sauce with a match, standing well back from the pan. Serve the crêpes on warmed plates. Fresh vanilla ice cream is a lovely accompaniment.

Chef's tip Leftover crêpes can be stacked, wrapped in foil and frozen in an airtight bag. To defrost, refrigerate them overnight, then peel off to use. They are a handy and very versatile stand-by.

Burgundy granita

A granita in Italian—or granité in French—is a close cousin to the true sorbet. It is made with sharp-tasting fruit, spiked with wine or champagne. Due to its low sugar content, small crystals form during freezing, giving the dessert its name: a granita should always give the impression of crushed ice.

*Preparation time **10 minutes + 3 hours freezing***
*Total cooking time **5 minutes***
Serves 8

175 g (5³/4 oz) caster sugar
80 ml (2³/4 fl oz) orange juice
2 tablespoons lime juice
1 tablespoon chopped lemon balm or mint
750 ml (24 fl oz) Burgundy or other red wine
sprigs of lemon balm or mint, to garnish

1 Chill eight serving glasses in the refrigerator. Place the sugar, orange juice, lime juice, lemon balm or mint and 130 ml (4¹/4 fl oz) water in a pan over medium heat. Ensuring the mixture doesn't boil, stir until the sugar has dissolved. Bring to the boil, reduce the heat and simmer for 2–3 minutes.

2 Strain the syrup through a fine wire sieve, allow it to cool thoroughly, then add the wine. Stir well and pour the mixture into a shallow, freezer-proof container. Freeze for 3 hours, or until set.

3 When it is fully frozen and crystallised, scrape the granita into the chilled glasses using a metal spoon. Decorate each glass with sprigs of lemon balm or mint and serve at once.

Oeufs à la neige

In English, this amazing dessert is better known as 'floating islands', or more literally
'snow eggs'. A rich custard sauce (crème anglaise) is topped with meltingly soft
meringues and drizzled with caramel sauce.

Preparation time **40 minutes**
Total cooking time **40 minutes**
Serves 6–8

SYRUP
185 g (6 oz) sugar

CREME ANGLAISE
500 ml (16 fl oz) milk
1 vanilla pod
6 egg yolks
125 g (4 oz) caster sugar

MERINGUES
6 egg whites
125 g (4 oz) caster sugar

CARAMEL SAUCE
100 g (3¹/4 oz) sugar
lemon juice, to taste

1 To make the syrup, dissolve the sugar in 2 litres water over low heat. Bring to the boil, then reduce the heat and leave to simmer gently.

2 To make the crème anglaise, prepare a large bowl of ice or iced water and place a smaller bowl inside. Place the milk and vanilla pod in a heavy-based pan, and just bring to the boil. Make the custard following the Chef's techniques on page 63, then strain into the prepared bowl in the ice. Leave to cool, stirring occasionally.

3 To make the meringues, beat the egg whites in a clean, dry bowl until stiff peaks form. Add the sugar and beat until smooth and glossy. Shape into 'eggs' using two large spoons dipped in water, then poach in the gently simmering syrup for 3 minutes, taking care not to crowd the pan. Turn using a slotted spoon and poach for 3 more minutes. Drain on a tea towel, and leave to cool.

4 To make the caramel sauce, place the sugar, 50 ml (1³/4 fl oz) water and a few drops of lemon juice in a heavy-based saucepan. Stir over low heat until the sugar dissolves. Simmer for about 4–5 minutes, or until the caramel just takes on a golden colour: the sauce should be thick and syrupy. Stop the cooking immediately by plunging the saucepan into a large, heatproof bowl of iced water for a few seconds. Remove the saucepan and keep the caramel warm or it will harden.

5 To serve, fill a shallow bowl with crème anglaise and top with poached meringues. Drizzle the caramel over and serve the remaining sauce in a sauce boat.

Baked apple and fruit charlotte

*As legend has it, this famous moulded dessert was named after the wife of George III,
England's famous 'mad' king. It is traditionally set in a tall, bucket-shaped mould.*

*Preparation time **30 minutes + 1 hour cooling***
*Total cooking time **1 hour 20 minutes***
*Serves **6***

14 thin slices of white bread, trimmed of crusts
175 g (5³⁄4 oz) unsalted butter
**500 g (1 lb) Granny Smith apples, peeled, cored and
    finely chopped**
**500 g (1 lb) cooking apples, peeled, cored and finely
    chopped**
90 g (3 oz) soft brown sugar
pinch of ground cinnamon
¹⁄2 teaspoon ground nutmeg
50 g (1³⁄4 oz) walnuts, finely chopped
50 g (1³⁄4 oz) sultanas or other dried fruits
2 tablespoons marmalade (optional)
grated lemon rind (optional)
3 tablespoons apricot jam (see Chef's tips)

1 Brush a 1.25 litre charlotte mould with softened
butter. Cut six slices of bread in half to form rectangles;
cut five slices in half at a diagonal to form triangles.
Reserve the remaining three slices of bread.

2 Turn the mould upside down and place the bread
triangles on top, overlapping the edges to completely
cover the top of the mould. Hold the triangles in place
and, using the mould as a guide, trim the excess edges
with scissors so the triangles will fit inside the base of
the mould exactly.

3 Melt 150 g (5 oz) of the butter, dip the trimmed
triangles in, then line the base of the mould. Dip the
rectangles in butter and arrange around the sides,
overlapping the edges until the mould is completely
covered, filling any gaps with the bread trimmings. Dip
the reserved slices of bread in the butter and set aside.

4 To make the filling, melt the remaining butter in a
large pan. Add the apples, cover the pan with baking
paper and then a lid. Cook the apples over low heat
for 15–20 minutes, or until they are soft and of the
consistency of apple sauce. Add the sugar and stir over
high heat for about 5 minutes, or until the mixture falls
from the side of the spoon in wide drops. Stir in the
cinnamon, nutmeg, walnuts and sultanas. Remove from
the heat. Add the marmalade, and perhaps a little grated
lemon rind. Set aside to cool.

5 Preheat the oven to moderately hot 190°C (375°F/
Gas 5). Ladle the filling into the mould until half full.
Cover the filling with half the reserved bread slices,
press down firmly, then add the remaining filling. If the
filling is not level with the mould lining, trim the bread
carefully with the tip of a small knife or scissors. Cover
with the remaining reserved bread, taking care to fill any
gaps. Press in gently and cover with foil.

6 Place the charlotte on a baking tray and bake for
45 minutes to 1 hour, or until golden and firm. Leave to
cool completely before turning out onto a serving plate:
this should take about 1 hour.

7 Warm the apricot jam and 25 ml (³⁄4 fl oz) water in a
small pan over low heat until melted. Brush the mixture
over the surface of the charlotte to give a light glaze.

Chef's tips A heatproof soufflé dish or cake tin can be
used instead of a charlotte mould.

　　If the jam is very fruity, it will be easier to brush onto
the charlotte if it has been strained after warming. An
inexpensive jam is fine for this purpose.

　　For extra zest, replace the sultanas with 1–2 tablespoons
chopped glacé ginger and the nutmeg with ground ginger.

　　For an indulgent accompaniment, whip 150 ml
(5 fl oz) whipping cream with 50 g (1³⁄4 oz) sugar, then
stir in 2 tablespoons of Calvados.

Gooseberry fool

England is the home of this old-fashioned but delicious dessert made of cooked, strained and puréed fruit, chilled and folded into custard and whipped cream. Traditionally, fool is made from gooseberries, although any fruit may be used.

*Preparation time **40 minutes + 2 hours refrigeration***
*Total cooking time **25 minutes***
*Serves **4–6***

GOOSEBERRY PUREE
120 g (4 oz) caster sugar
500 g (1 lb) fresh gooseberries, topped and tailed
1 leaf gelatine or 1/2 teaspoon gelatine powder

1 1/2 tablespoons cornflour
3 tablespoons caster sugar
125 ml (4 fl oz) milk
125 ml (4 fl oz) Greek or plain thick yoghurt
75 ml (2 1/2 fl oz) cream, for whipping
1 egg white
100 ml (3 1/4 fl oz) cream for whipping, to serve
4–6 macaroon biscuits, to serve

1 To make the purée, reserve 1 tablespoon of sugar and place the rest in a heavy-based pan with 250 ml (8 fl oz) water. Stir over low heat until the sugar dissolves. Bring to the boil, add the fruit, reduce the heat and simmer for 10 minutes, or until tender. Strain the liquid. Purée the fruit in a food processor, then stir in the reserved sugar.
2 Soak the gelatine leaf or powder, following the Chef's techniques on page 63.
3 In a separate heatproof bowl, combine the cornflour and 1 tablespoon of the sugar. Add 50 ml (1 3/4 fl oz) of the milk and stir until smooth. Bring the remaining milk almost to the boil, then whisk it into the cornflour and sugar. Place in a clean pan and whisk over low heat until the mixture boils and thickens. Remove from the heat.
4 Stir the soaked gelatine into the hot custard until dissolved, then cover with baking paper and leave to cool. Stir in the fruit purée and yoghurt, mixing well.
5 Whip the cream until soft peaks form, then fold into the custard. Whisk the egg white in a clean, dry bowl until stiff, then whisk in the remaining sugar and fold into the custard. Pipe or spoon the fool into tall glasses, ensuring there are no air pockets. Chill for 2 hours to set. Serve with freshly whipped cream and macaroons.

Chef's tip If the gooseberries are tart, sweeten them with a little sugar. Frozen gooseberries may be used in this recipe if fresh ones are not available.

Cabinet puddings

In this classic English dessert, leftover sponge cake is transformed into a scrumptious treat, often soaked in liqueur, dressed with dried fruit and custard, then baked in individual flower-pot shaped moulds. Cabinet pudding is usually served with fresh vanilla custard.

*Preparation time **35 minutes***
*Total cooking time **1 hour 20 minutes***
Serves 4

caster sugar, for dusting
100 g (3¹/4 oz) sponge cake
1 tablespoon glacé cherries, chopped
2 tablespoons currants
3 tablespoons sultanas
3 teaspoons Kirsch
2 eggs
1¹/2 tablespoons caster sugar
¹/2 teaspoon vanilla extract or essence
250 ml (8 fl oz) milk

1 Preheat the oven to slow 150°C (300°F/Gas 2). Lightly brush four 160 ml (5¹/4 fl oz) dariole moulds or ramekins with softened butter. Place some sugar in a mould and, without placing your fingers inside the mould, rotate it so that a layer of sugar adheres to the butter. Tap out any excess sugar and repeat with the other moulds.

2 Cut the sponge cake into 5 mm (¹/4 inch) cubes and mix in a bowl with the glacé cherries, currants and sultanas. Pour the Kirsch over, toss lightly, then leave to soak for a few minutes. Divide the cake and fruit mixture between the four moulds.

3 Beat the eggs lightly in a large heatproof bowl and whisk in the sugar and vanilla extract or essence. Warm the milk in a small, heavy-based pan until bubbles show around the edge of the pan. Follow the method for making custard in the Chef's techniques on page 63, then pour the custard into each of the moulds.

4 Half fill a baking dish or deep ovenproof dish with hot water, place the moulds inside and set aside for 5 minutes. Bake for 1 hour, or until the puddings are just firm to the light touch of a finger. Remove from the oven and cool for 3–4 minutes before turning out onto a warm serving dish. Serve with vanilla custard.

Gratin of fruits

Gratins are grilled until golden, giving a glorious, appetising colour. Here, a warm, rich sabayon provides a sensational topping to a simple medley of fresh fruit.

Preparation time **30 minutes**
Total cooking time **25–30 minutes**
Serves 4

2 peaches

2 nectarines

2 plums

4 lychees

2 passion fruit

250 g (8 oz) strawberries

250 g (8 oz) raspberries

2 eggs, plus 2 egg yolks

80 g (2³/4 oz) caster sugar

3 teaspoons Kirsch

fresh mint leaves, to decorate

1 Wash the peaches, nectarines and plums and dry them well. Cut the fruits in half, then twist the two halves in opposite directions to separate them. Remove the stones and thinly slice the fruits.

2 Peel away the tough brittle skin of the lychees. Slit each fruit down one side through to the stone, then open the flesh and remove the stone. Cut the passion fruit in half, scooping the pulp and seeds into a bowl. Rinse the strawberries and pull out the stalks. Arrange all the fruit decoratively on four heatproof plates or individual shallow dishes, then spoon the passion fruit pulp and seeds over the top.

3 Heat the grill to a high setting. Fill a pan with enough water so that the bottom of the bowl used in the next step does not touch the simmering water when placed over it. Bring the water to the boil, then reduce the heat to a simmer.

4 Place the eggs, yolks and sugar in a large heatproof bowl, then place the bowl over the pan of simmering water. Whisk for 10–15 minutes, or until the mixture becomes thick and creamy and leaves a trail as it falls from the whisk. Stir in the Kirsch.

5 Spoon the sauce over the fruit and grill quickly until the sabayon is an even brown. Decorate with mint leaves and serve.

Chef's tip The fruit plates can be prepared beforehand and covered with plastic wrap to prevent the fruit drying out.

Apple fritters

The apples in this classic favourite can be replaced with almost any fruit that cooks well. Bananas, pineapple and pears are perfect substitutes.

*Preparation time **35 minutes***
*Total cooking time **20 minutes***
*Serves **6–8***

900 g (1 lb 13 oz) Golden Delicious apples
140 g (4¹/2 oz) caster sugar
100 ml (3¹/4 fl oz) Calvados
300 g (10 oz) plain flour
2 tablespoons potato starch or cornflour
2 eggs, plus 4 egg whites
250 ml (8 fl oz) beer
oil, for deep-frying
50 g (1³/4 oz) icing sugar, to dust

1 Peel and core the apples, then slice them into 1 cm (1/2 inch) rounds so that each has a hole in the centre. Combine 100 g (3¹/4 oz) of the sugar with the Calvados and use it to coat the apple. Set aside.

2 Sift the flour, starch and a pinch of salt into a large bowl. Make a well in the centre and whisk in the two eggs, the beer and then 1 tablespoon oil. Mix to a smooth, lump-free batter and set aside to rest. (The batter will be very thick, to coat and cook the apples.) Fill a large deep pan or deep fryer one third full of oil. Preheat to 170°C (325°F).

3 Beat the egg whites until soft peaks form, then add the remaining sugar. Beat until smooth and glossy. Fold into the batter with a large metal spoon.

4 Drain the apples on paper towels. Dip the slices in batter one at a time and deep-fry. Once browned, turn and cook the other side. Remove and drain on paper towels. Serve warm or hot, sprinkled with icing sugar.

Crêpes soufflées

An old French custom when cooking crêpes is to make a wish while flipping the crêpe, holding a coin in the hand for prosperity. Your guests will feel blessed indeed when offered this ambrosial dessert.

*Preparation time **40 minutes + 1 hour resting***
*Total cooking time **15 minutes***
Makes 9 crêpes

CREPE BATTER
2 tablespoons sugar
75 g (2 1/2 oz) plain flour
1 egg, lightly beaten
200 ml (6 1/2 fl oz) milk
1/4 teaspoon vanilla extract or essence

unsalted butter, for cooking

SOUFFLE FILLING
225 ml (7 1/4 fl oz) milk
1/4 vanilla pod, split lengthways
125 g (4 oz) sugar
4 egg yolks
2 tablespoons cornflour
1–2 teaspoons Grand Marnier
5 egg whites

1 To make the crêpes, sift the sugar, flour and a pinch of salt into a bowl. Make a well in the centre and add the egg. Whisk briskly to draw in the flour, slowly adding half the milk in a thin steady stream. Whisk until smooth. Add the vanilla and remaining milk, whisking constantly into a smooth batter—you may need to sieve the batter to remove all the lumps. Cover with plastic wrap and rest for at least 1 hour, preferably overnight.
2 Over medium heat, melt some butter in a 16–18 cm (6 1/2–7 inch) heavy-based or non-stick pan; pour out any excess butter. Stir the batter well and pour into the pan from a ladle or jug, starting in the centre and swirling the pan to create a thin coating. Cook for 1 minute, or until bubbles appear, the batter sets and the edges are brown. Carefully loosen and lift the edges with a palette knife or spatula. Turn and cook for 30 seconds, or until lightly golden. Remove from the pan with the first-fried side facing down. Set aside. Repeat with the remaining batter. When cooled, lightly sprinkle the crêpes with sugar and stack them, separated with greaseproof paper. Preheat the oven to moderate 180°C (350°F/Gas 4).
3 To make the soufflé filling, slowly bring the milk and vanilla pod to the boil in a medium pan. Remove from the heat and set aside for 3 minutes to infuse the milk. In a separate bowl, vigorously beat the sugar and egg yolks with a wire whisk until pale. Stir in the cornflour, gradually pour in the scalded milk and return the mixture to the pan. Stir for 2–3 minutes over moderate heat, or until thickened. Stir in the Grand Marnier, cover with baking paper and set aside to cool.
4 Remove the vanilla pod from the custard. In a separate bowl, whisk the egg whites until stiff peaks form. Using a large metal spoon, fold the egg whites into the custard in at least three batches. Gently fold until the mixture is well combined: it should be light and airy.
5 Place some filling on one half of the paler side of the crêpes. Fold over into a semicircle, but do not seal the edges. Place on a lightly greased oven tray and bake for 10–15 minutes. The crêpes will open slightly. Using a wide spatula, carefully place each crêpe onto a warm serving plate. The crêpes may be served with a chocolate or fruit sauce, but are also delicious on their own.

Chef's tip If the first crêpes stick, the pan may not be hot enough. Always present crêpes with the first-cooked side facing outwards: it is more nicely browned with a lovely lace-like pattern.

Chef's techniques

◆

Clarifying butter

Removing the water and solids from butter makes it less likely to burn. Ghee is a form of clarified butter.

To make 100 g (3¼ oz) clarified butter, cut 180 g (5¾ oz) butter into small cubes. Place in a small pan set into a larger pot of water over low heat. Melt the butter without stirring.

Remove the pan from the heat and allow to cool slightly. Skim the foam from the surface, being careful not to stir the butter.

Pour off the clear yellow liquid, being very careful to leave the milky sediment behind in the pan. Discard the sediment and store the clarified butter in an airtight container in the refrigerator.

Baking blind

Baking the pastry before adding the filling prevents the base becoming soggy during cooking.

After the pastry has been eased into the prepared tin, use a small ball of excess pastry to gently press the pastry into the sides of the tin around the fluted edges.

Use a rolling pin to trim the pastry edges. Gently but firmly roll across the top of the tin. Refrigerate for 10 minutes.

Prick the pastry shell to allow steam to escape during baking. Line with crumpled greaseproof or baking paper, fill with rice or baking beans and bake for the time specified in the recipe.

Remove the paper and the hot rice or baking beans. Discard the paper. The rice or beans can be stored and used over and over again after cooking.

Making custard

Slow cooking and gentle heat are required to prevent the custard curdling.

Whisk the hot, infused milk or cream into the beaten eggs and sugar. Pour into a clean pan.

Stir gently over low heat with a wooden spoon for 10–15 minutes, or until the custard coats the back of the spoon and leaves
a clear parting when a finger is drawn across. Do not boil,

Strain the warm custard through a fine sieve into a
clean jug to remove any lumps.

Making a soufflé ridge

A successful soufflé has a high 'cap' in the centre, just like a traditional chef's cap.

Run your thumb around the inside of the soufflé dish. The ridge this creates will help the soufflé rise evenly.

Making Italian meringue

Close-textured and shiny, this meringue holds up well for up to two days without cooking.

Boil without stirring until the syrup reaches the soft-ball stage, 116–118°C (241–244°F). If you do not have a sugar thermometer, drop 1/4 teaspoon of the syrup into iced water: it should hold its shape

In a large heatproof bowl, beat the egg whites into soft peaks, using a balloon whisk or electric beaters. Avoiding the whisk, add the hot syrup in a thin steady stream, beating constantly until thick and glossy. Beat until cold.

Using gelatine

Leaf gelatine has no flavour or colour, gives a softer set than gelatine powder, and is easier to use.

Lower the leaves or sheets of gelatine into a bowl of cold water, adding each leaf separately to prevent sticking. Leave to soak for a few minutes, or until softened.

When the leaf is soft and pliable, carefully remove it and squeeze out any excess liquid. If you are using gelatine powder, dissolve each teaspoon of gelatine in 1 tablespoon of water, following the manufacturer's instructions.

Published by Bay Books, an imprint of Murdoch Books Pty Limited.

Murdoch Books and Le Cordon Bleu thank the 32 masterchefs of all the Le Cordon Bleu Schools, whose knowledge and expertise have made this book possible, especially: Chef Cliche (MOF), Chef Terrien, Chef Boucheret, Chef Duchêne (MOF), Chef Guillut, Chef Steneck, Paris; Chef Males, Chef Walsh, Chef Hardy, London; Chef Chantefort, Chef Bertin, Chef Jambert, Chef Honda, Tokyo; Chef Salembien, Chef Boutin, Chef Harris, Sydney; Chef Lawes, Adelaide; Chef Guiet, Chef Denis, Ottawa. Of the many students who helped the Chefs test each recipe, a special mention to graduates David Welch and Allen Wertheim.
A very special acknowledgment to Directors Susan Eckstein, Great Britain, and Kathy Shaw, Paris, who have been responsible for the coordination of the Le Cordon Bleu team throughout this series.

Murdoch Books Australia
Pier 8/9, 23 Hickson Rd,
Millers Point NSW 2000
Phone: +61 2 8220 2000
Fax: +61 2 8220 2558

Murdoch Books UK Limited
Erico House, 6th Floor North,
93-99 Upper Richmond Road
Putney, London SW15 2TG
Phone: +44 (0)20 8785 5995
Fax: +44 (0)20 8785 5985

ISBN-13: 978-1-921259-17-3
ISBN-10: 1-921259-17-5

Printed by SNP Leefung Printers Limited.
PRINTED IN CHINA.

This edition first published in 2006.

©Design and photography Murdoch Books 1997
©Text Le Cordon Bleu 1997

The Publisher and Le Cordon Bleu wish to thank Carole Sweetnam for her help with this series.
Front cover: Thin shortbreads with fresh cream and fruit.

IMPORTANT INFORMATION

CONVERSION GUIDE

1 cup = 250 ml (8 fl oz)
1 Australian tablespoon = 20 ml (4 teaspoons)
1 UK tablespoon = 15 ml (3 teaspoons)

NOTE: We have used 20 ml tablespoons. If you are using a 15 ml tablespoon, for most recipes the difference will be negligible. For recipes using baking powder, gelatine, bicarbonate of soda and flour, add an extra teaspoon for each tablespoon specified.

CUP CONVERSIONS—DRY INGREDIENTS

1 cup flour, plain or self-raising = 125 g (4 oz)
1 cup sugar, caster = 250 g (8 oz)
1 cup breadcrumbs, dry = 125 g (4 oz)

IMPORTANT: Those who might be at risk from the effects of salmonella food poisoning (the elderly, pregnant women, young children and those suffering from immune deficiency diseases) should consult their GP with any concerns about eating raw eggs.

Anne Frank
1929-1945

Contents

Introduction

Anne Frank, a young Jewish girl, was born in Germany in 1929. She experienced the growth of anti-Semitism during the 1930s. Fleeing with her family to apparent safety in the Netherlands, she was later caught up in the terrible persecution of the Jews by the Nazis in World War Two.

Anne's diary gives us an insight into what it was like to be Jewish in Europe at the time of the Second World War. By the end of that war, at least six million Jews had been killed. To understand how this could have happened, it is important to know how life changed in Germany after 1918.

Millions of soldiers worldwide were killed during World War One (1914–18). For Germans, the war was even more disastrous – after their country's defeat it had to pay huge reparations (sums of money) to its allied opponents – France, Britain and America. In addition, Germany's head of state, Kaiser Wilhelm II, went into exile in Belgium in 1918, where he lived until his death in 1941.

These events destabilized Germany, both economically and politically. Out of this instability a dictator in the person of Adolf Hitler emerged. As he rose to power Hitler manipulated public opinion. First he obtained power by democratic means; later he ruthlessly crushed democracy to ensure his own power as the leader of a new "German Empire".

Germany and World War One

By the end of the 19th century, Germany had become one of the strongest military and industrial powers in the world. The increased might and ambition of Germany threatened the older European countries (France, Russia and Great Britain). Growing tension came to a head when Archduke Franz Ferdinand, heir to the throne of Austria-Hungary, was assassinated in 1914. Russia jumped to the defence of Serbia, who were accused of sponsoring the killing, while Germany did the same for Austria-Hungary. Soon, other world powers were brought into the conflict. The war lasted for four years, ending with Germany's defeat in 1918.

Growing up in Frankfurt

Anne Frank was born on 12 June 1929 in the prosperous German city of Frankfurt am Main. Her full given name was Annelies Marie Frank.

At the time Frankfurt was an important commercial centre with a history dating back to medieval times. The city had always boasted a large Jewish population and in the year of Anne's birth, there were about 30,000 Jews out of a total population of 540,000.

The "new liberalism"

At the beginning of the 19th century Frankfurt's Jewish ghetto, the *Judengasse*, had been demolished and laws were passed to give equal rights to the Jewish population. Jews were free to integrate or live a traditional way of life as they chose. A symbol of this "new liberalism" was the building of the Borneplatz Synagogue in 1882, in a thriving, popular section next to the huge open-air market. By the end

▶ *Margot (left) and Anne with their father Otto in 1930. Anne was one year old.*

Otto's war service for Germany

Otto, together with his brothers Robert and Herbert, were among the estimated 100,000 German Jews who fought for Germany in World War One. As a lieutenant, Otto Frank outranked Corporal Hitler. Had the two men been members of the same unit, Hitler would have been in the position of having to take orders from Otto.

of the 19th century new industrial areas had grown on the east and west side of the city. By 1918 Frankfurt had overrun its neighbouring villages to become the largest German city in land area.

Otto and Edith Frank

Anne's father, Otto, was born in the affluent Westend area of the city in 1889. His parents belonged to the Liberal Jewish congregation and had friends of different faiths and backgrounds. Although anti-Semitism had been rife in Frankfurt for centuries, Otto later claimed that he never encountered an anti-Semite in his youth in Frankfurt. At the age of 19, after finishing high school and studying art history at Heidelberg University for just one term, Otto was offered work in Macy's department store in New York City. He jumped at the chance to travel and soon grew to love New York. However, after the death of his father, he returned to Germany in 1909. Back home, he found work with an engineering company in Düsseldorf, until the outbreak of World War One in 1914.

Anne's mother, Edith Holländer was born and grew up in Aachen, close to the Belgian and Dutch border, where her father worked in manufacturing. Otto and Edith met through the Franks' business and were married in 1925. Otto was 36 and Edith was 25. Although they were not madly in love, they had much in common. On 16 February, 1926, Anne's elder sister Margot Betti Frank was born.

The Jewish ghettos

Many Jews had settled in Germany in the Middle Ages, seeking refuge from persecution in other parts of Europe. The Jewish Ghetto, which had its beginnings in 16th-century Italy, was an isolated area of town set aside for the Jewish community. Pope Paul IV granted the Jews protection from persecution on the understanding that they paid taxes. Many ghettos were thriving places, where the skills of Jewish merchants and tradesmen added to the overall prosperity of the town.

By June 1929, the month in which Anne was born, Otto was well established, working for his father's bank in Frankfurt. Anne's family belonged to the wealthy middle classes, which had solid roots in Germany and had fought for their country in World War One.

In the early part of the twentieth century, Frankfurt was a reasonably tolerant place, but throughout the 1920s there was frequent unrest and the large Jewish population often found themselves under threat of attack from the National Socialists (the Nazis), an extreme, nationalistic political party that blamed Jews and Communists for Germany's defeat in World War One. Despite this strand of anti-Semitism, business was good and life was comfortable for the Frank family.

Anne's early years

The first years of Anne's life were spent in happy circumstances. In 1931 the family moved to 24 Ganghoferstrasse, an up-and-coming neighbourhood known as the Poets' Quarter. Otto Frank, a keen amateur photographer, took numerous photographs of Anne and Margot playing at home and with friends, and on family holidays and outings. An early photo of Anne shows her in hospital, a one-day-old baby in her mother's arms. Other photos record the loving relationship between the sisters in early childhood, time spent with their grandparents, and visits from their close cousins, Stephan and Buddy. As they grew up, the girls' individual characters emerged: Margot was kind-hearted and shy and looked very much like her mother; Anne was lively, funny, and outgoing, more like her father. As the slightly spoilt younger daughter, she was her "daddy's girl". Both girls adored their father, who often told them bedtime stories about two girls named Paula, one good and one mischievous.

Economic slump

On 24 October 1929 (a day later referred to as Black Thursday), America's stock market collapsed. The "Wall Street Crash" ushered in an economic slump, a period known as the Great Depression, which lasted until the beginning of the Second World War in 1939. For Germany, still paying huge debts from the 1914–18 war, this was a disaster. The government (the National Assembly) began to lose control, leaving only the German Labour

Movement and various left-wing groups to oppose Adolf Hitler's popular right-wing Nazi Party, who promised a great German revival.

In the year of Anne's birth, German banknotes became practically worthless and in Frankfurt, by the end of 1932, more than 70,000 workers were unemployed. Trade union membership in Germany reached 12 million; the unions began to demand that the government introduce rationing of essentials to help control the economic crisis. The situation became so bad that the desperate German people began to look to extremists for solutions to their problems. As a result, the Nazi Party began to recruit more and more followers. At first, Hitler blamed

▼ *Throughout the 1920s, as the economic situation in Germany worsened, the dole queues grew longer.*

Propaganda and "spin"

The Nazis were the first political party to use propaganda to manipulate the public and justify their actions. Putting a "spin" on real facts and statistics to encourage people to agree with your point of view is not uncommon in politics today. This manipulation of the truth was so important to the Nazis that they formulated very disciplined methods of communicating with the public, through printed material (like this romanticized illustration of Hitler), radio broadcasts and mass rallies.

the government for being weak. Later, he accused the Jews of not only causing but also exploiting the terrible German economic situation to their advantage, at the expense of "honest German people". Hitler's selection of the Jews as scapegoats happened at a time when many people were looking for someone to blame for their misfortune. His twisted views, expressed in his book *Mein Kampf* (*My Struggle*), together with his political ambitions, proved to be horribly effective. As his party gathered support, Jews found that their position within German society was becoming untenable.

In the September 1930 elections Hitler's Nazi Party became the second-largest party. The number of people who had voted for the Nazis had increased from 800,000 in 1928 to nearly 6.5 million. On 11 October 1931 Germany's right-wing political parties joined together to demand new elections. The following year, general elections were held and Hitler won 37 per cent of the 13.5 million vote. At first he headed a coalition government, but later he

◀ *Adolf Hitler's Nazi party rose to prominence with promises to make Germany great again. This poster portrays Hitler as the leader of the German people.*

Nazi thug tactics

Nazis did not just use "spin" and propaganda to gain power. They also used brute force. In 1921 Hitler had founded the SA division of the Nazi party, also known as the Storm Troopers or Brownshirts. They were his assault troops, made up mainly of ex-soldiers and other militant, rough characters. The SA carried out street assaults on German Jews and Nazi opponents, and intimidated voters during elections. The SA played a key role in Hitler's rise to power.

exploited the divided opposition to become Chancellor (Prime Minister) of Germany in January 1933.

In Frankfurt, two months later, the Nazi Party received a large share of the council votes. Nazi supporters gathered outside the town hall, raising their hands in the Nazi salute as they shouted, "Heil Hitler! Down with the Jews!". The same month saw hundreds arrested as the Nazis rounded up their political opponents and stepped up their repression of the Jews.

▶ *When the Franks lived there, Frankfurt was a bustling cosmopolitan city. This is a view from the mid-1930s.*

From Germany to Holland

On 5 March 1933 the German people voted again. This time, the Nazi party won 44 per cent of the vote and on 23 March the Enabling Law was passed.

This new law allowed Hitler to ignore the constitution and ratify any law he cared to make. On 14 July all other political parties were declared illegal – Hitler's power was absolute. Served by a close circle of associates, which included Joseph Goebbels, Hermann Goering, Heinrich Himmler and Reinhard Heydrich, he declared Germany to be the Third Reich (Empire).

Hitler crushes opposition

Hitler's first political acts removed or suppressed any opposition. The German Labour movement was one of his first targets. During March 1933, 10,000 active trade union members were arrested and in May of that year the leaders of the unions were replaced by Nazi Party members. All workers were now forced to join the DAF (German Workers Front), which was controlled by the Nazis. Employers and their workers were forced to co-operate with Hitler's government; strikes were not tolerated. At Oranienburg, near Berlin, a "concentration camp" was built to hold opponents to the Nazi regime. In 1933 150,000 people were sent there for so-called "re-education".

German churches soon endorsed the Nazis' political and racial policies. There were a few exceptions, but on 28 March 1933, Catholic bishops lifted their ban on parishioners becoming members of the Nazi Party. Persecution of the Jews and other minorities went on without a word of protest from the official churches. Only the Bekennende church,

▶ *The Nazis relied on elaborate rallies to maintain power by fear, as here at Nuremburg in 1938 .*

a Protestant group, objected to the outrageous injustices from the outset.

Isolating Jewish people

In Frankfurt, the Jewish mayor was replaced by a Nazi, and a swastika flag – the official Nazi symbol – was raised above the city's town hall. In April 1933 Joseph Goebbels, now Minister for Propaganda, declared an official boycott of all Jewish teachers, doctors, lawyers and shopkeepers. Later that month all civil servants with Jewish ancestry were fired from their jobs. Apart from these official acts, dozens of obstructive measures were used to make sure that life quickly became impossible for the majority of Jews in Germany. Nazi philosophy stated that there was only room in the country for Aryan (pure-bred white) Germans. Jewish business owners were forced to sell to their Aryan countrymen at knockdown prices and to witness the dismissal of any Jewish staff.

It was most likely during the first months of 1933 that Otto Frank began to consider leaving his country. When Hitler became Chancellor of Germany,

◀ *Another Nuremburg rally, this time of the Nazi Party's youth wing, or "Hitler Youth", in 1933.*

there were about 500,000 Jews living in the cities and throughout the countryside. As the various decrees against them mounted, increasingly isolating them from the rest of the population, many Jews who could afford to leave Germany did so.

Most fled with nothing, taking up work in the clothing or diamond industries in other European countries, America or Britain. Otto's sister Leni and her husband Erich, together with their children Stephan and Buddy, left in 1933. The same year Otto's mother went to Basel, Switzerland to join her daughter. By now Jews were not recognized as German citizens and their children were excluded from schools attended by non-Jews. This meant that Anne was unable to go to the nursery of her parents' choice and Margot had to leave the school she loved. Otto and Edith were only too aware of the worsening situation.

The move to Amsterdam

There were several reasons why Otto Frank chose to take his family to Holland. He had friends there, it was familiar and, perhaps more importantly, Dutch policy on refugees was more liberal than in most other countries. In World War One, Holland and Switzerland had been neutral. Both countries expected to remain neutral even if a new war broke out. So, when his brother-in-law arranged for him to work in the Dutch office of his company in Amsterdam, Otto grabbed the opportunity to get his family out of Germany. In 1933, as the Nazi Party gathered support, the Franks were among 63,000 Jews to leave. Anne and Margot stayed with their grandmother in Aachen until their parents were settled. Margot joined her parents in Amsterdam in December 1933 and Anne followed in February 1934. Early on in her diary Anne explained that when she arrived in Amsterdam, "I was plonked down on the table as a birthday present for Margot."

In Amsterdam, Otto soon became Managing Director of the Opekta Company, which manufactured spices and pectin, used in jam-making. The family moved into a house on Merwedeplein in Amsterdam's River Quarter and Anne and Margot attended the local Montessori school. They made friends both at school and with other Jewish immigrant families living nearby.

Fascism appears in Holland

Even in Holland, traditionally a liberal nation, the fascist movement had gained a foothold. In 1931 Anton Mussert founded the National Socialist Movement (NSB), which was modelled on the German Nazi Party. Many people who had no faith in the main political parties in the Netherlands joined this new right-wing group. A year after Anne arrived in Amsterdam, a general election was held and the National Socialist Movement obtained 8 per cent of the votes cast. Otto and Edith Frank must have been relieved when, in 1936, the NSB's popularity started to wane. This was due to its anti-Semitism and the fact that its leadership did not have the ruthlessness of its German counterpart.

Events back in Germany

The years between 1934 and 1940 were secure and happy for the Franks in the Netherlands. However, in Germany, the Nazis were consolidating their hold. Anne's parents were determined to keep news of the worsening situation from their children for as long as possible.

During the 1930s, further laws were introduced to authorize the forced sterilization of any individual deemed likely to produce "genetically unfit" offspring. Laws forbidding marriage between Jews and non-Jews were passed in 1935, and in 1937 Hitler's secret state police, the *Gestapo*, took nearly 400 black and mixed-race German children to hospital for sterilization. In 1939 Anne's maternal grandmother moved from Aachen to join the family in Amsterdam.

German laws to isolate Jews

By 1938 Jews had no legal rights at all. Hitler showed how simple it was to isolate a people in their own country.

- German children were forbidden to speak to Jews
- Jews who had passports were ordered to hand them in
- Jewish property was confiscated and businesses closed down
- Jews were forbidden to deal in property, jewellery or precious metals or freely operate bank accounts
- In Munich, Jews were given 48 hours to leave or else go to concentration camps

The "Night of broken glass"

On 9–10 November, 1938 the event that became known as "*Kristallnacht*" or "Night of broken glass" took place. Dozens of synagogues, including Frankfurt's

▶ *A woman surveys damage to a Jewish shop in Berlin as a result of Kristallnacht, 9-10 November 1938.*

▲ *Kristallnacht damage was not confined to Jewish businesses. This is the interior of the Okel Jaakov synagogue in Munich on 10 November 1938.*

Borneplatz, and thousands of Jewish shops in Germany and Austria were broken into and set on fire. During this night of outrage, which left shattered glass on the streets, German men and women were seen jeering at Jews and encouraging their attackers.

Then on 12 November, around 30,000 Jewish men and boys were arrested and taken to Dachau, Buchenwald and Sachsenhausen concentration camps. This was the first deadly step on the path towards what the Nazis were to call "The Final Solution".

21

Invasion of Holland

Adolf Hitler secured the support of the German armed forces early on in his "reign of terror". He pandered to their sense of pride, reminding them about the loss of German territory after World War One and the need to erase the shame of their country's defeat.

Hitler planned to regain former German territories and expand the German border east to gain new "living space" (referred to as *Lebensraum*). The military agreed to support him only if he limited the brutal power of the two and a half million-strong SA or Brownshirts. On 30 June 1934 the SA leaders were murdered on Hitler's orders and at the end of the same year the German army swore allegiance directly to Hitler.

Germany begins invasions

Rearmament started in 1934, and by the middle of 1935 military conscription was reintroduced. In 1938, the German army invaded Czechoslovakia and the old German territory of the Sudetenland. Hitler's next target was Poland and despite Britain's threat to go to war with Germany if Hitler invaded, the Germans crossed into Polish territory in September 1939. This invasion was the spark that ignited World War Two.

The Maginot Line

As in World War One, France and Britain were allied against Germany. Since 1918 the French had built an enormous fortified line with massive gun emplacements, subterranean armouries and barracks for the troops who manned it. Known as the Maginot Line, it was believed to be proof against any German attack. The northern end of the Maginot Line terminated at the Belgian border.

▶ *A view of Amsterdam in the 1930s.*

23

For the first nine months after war was declared, an uneasy silence settled across Europe – this period was known as the "Phoney War". By 1940 Holland had absorbed about 24,000 Jewish refugees, swelling the total population of Jews living there to 140,000, of which 90,000 were living in Amsterdam. This city now held the largest Jewish population in Europe.

On 10 May 1940 the Germans surprised everyone by launching an attack on the Netherlands. Dutch neutrality had been violated and the Maginot Line rendered useless as a defence for France. The Germans dropped paratroopers and quickly seized all the key areas of the country within a few days. Brisk fighting forced the Dutch government and royal family to flee to Britain. On 15 May 1940, Holland capitulated. This followed the bombing of Rotterdam, during which more than 900 people were killed and 24,000 houses destroyed. The country was now under German occupation.

"Blitzkrieg"

Throughout the summer months of 1940 the German occupying forces in Holland were careful not to antagonize the Dutch people. This was because the German army was engaged in its "Blitzkrieg" campaign across Belgium and northern France. When the French army realized that the Maginot Line provided no defence and French troops were cut off by the Germans' rapid advance, they gave up. The British had been forced to retreat to the French coast, where an extraordinary rescue took place at Dunkirk. An armada of small civilian boats turned up and took the troops off the beaches and safely back to England.

The display of German military supremacy heralded new laws in the Netherlands. These included the imposition of the black-out, issuing of ration cards and, in May 1941, compulsory carrying of identity cards.

In the autumn of 1940 the Nazis took the first step towards persecution of the Jews in Holland. A "Declaration of Aryanism" form was presented to civil servants, judges, employers and teachers asking if any of their parents or grandparents were Jewish. Almost the entire population of the country filled in these forms, and the information provided made the next stages of the Jewish persecution easy.

▲ *German aircraft, loaded with paratroops, launch the first wave of the assault on Holland on 10 May 1940.*

Persecuting Jews in Holland

As in Germany, between 1933 and 1938, anti-Jewish measures were taken in Holland increasingly to isolate Jews.

In February 1941 Mussert's paramilitary arm of the NSB, the Weer-Afdeling, entered Amsterdam's Jewish quarter, deliberately provoking trouble by raiding the markets on Amstelveld and Waterloo Square. Heavy fighting followed when

25

▼ *A column of German cavalry advances through a Dutch village in 1940.*

organized Jewish groups defended their property. One of the Weer-Afdeling militants was killed in a skirmish and the German forces used this as an excuse to retaliate. The Jewish quarter was

sealed off on 22 February and 400 men and boys were rounded up, beaten and held in Jonas Daniel Meijer Square before being taken away – never to be seen again.

Protests and resistance

On 26 February tens of thousands of people took part in a general strike in and around Amsterdam to protest against the seizing of the 400 innocent people. The next day German troops broke up the

strike, firing live rounds of ammunition and arresting people indiscriminately. The strike ended when the people realized the Nazis had no qualms about further reprisals if the strike continued. Several months later death notices reached relatives of those taken in the February round-up, stating that the arrested men and boys had been killed in Mauthausen concentration camp.

Although the majority of the Dutch population were anti-Nazi, a large minority collaborated with the Germans. These were members of the various national socialist organizations, such as Mussert's NSB. The Dutch Union (NU) was founded to provide a focus of protest against German Nazism, but it also looked for ways to co-operate with the German authorities so that it could maintain its independence. In 1941, following its protest against anti-Jewish laws, the NU was banned. The Union had learned, to its cost, that the Nazis were not interested in compromise.

By 1942 most of the anti-Jewish decrees were in place. Anne listed them

◀ *The Nazis forced Dutch Jews – such as these people in Amsterdam – to wear a yellow star with the word* Jood *(Jew) on it.*

in her diary entry for 20 June 1942. They match those in place in Germany in the years between 1933 and 1938. Jews were required to wear a yellow cloth star with the word *Jood* on their clothes. They had to hand in their bicycles to the authorities and were forbidden to use trams or ride in cars, even if the car was their own. Jewish children were banned from state schools and were forced to attend special Jewish ones. Jews had to do their shopping between 3.00 and 5.00 p.m., and were required to go to Jewish-owned barbers and beauty salons. They were forbidden to go to theatres, cinemas or other forms of entertainment and were banned from using sporting facilities or taking part in any athletic activity in public. Jews had to observe a curfew and were not allowed out on the streets or even into their own gardens after 8.00 p.m. They were forbidden to visit Christians in their homes. These restrictions were designed to segregate the Jews from the rest of Dutch society. But they also fanned anti-Semitic feeling, encouraging Dutch Christians to regard Jews as outsiders who posed a dangerous threat to the so-called "Dutch Aryan" way of life.

The diary

Soon after arriving in Holland, Anne began her schooling. In the spring of 1934 she started at a Montessori nursery school, which was close to the Franks' house on Merwedeplein.

Anne was a promising pupil and at the age of seven was already reading and writing well. If Anne seemed to be a good student, her elder sister Margot was definitely the scholar of the family. Anne later recorded in her diary: "Margot has also got her report. Brilliant as usual. If we had such a thing as 'cum laude', she would have passed with honours."

At the Montessori school Anne had both Jewish and Christian friends. She was attractive and popular, regarding herself as a bit of a clown. Among her early close friends were Sanne Ledermann and Hanneli Goslar. As a trio, the girls were known as "Anne, Hanne and Sanne". Hanneli (Lies) later recalled how Anne would entertain her classmates and make them laugh. She could dislocate her shoulder at will, a trick she enjoyed

▶ The Nazis wasted no time in strengthening their grip on Holland. This picture shows the Reichskommisar (governor) of the Netherlands, Arthur Seyss-Inquart, watching a parade of Nazi military police in Amsterdam on 10 February 1941.

performing to an appreciative audience. Lies also acknowledged Anne's early literary promise, saying that her writing was "very mature" for her age.

In the summer of 1941, as a result of German orders demanding segregation of Christians and Jews in Holland, Anne was accepted at the Jewish Lyceum, which her sister Margot was attending. Anne recorded her emotional farewell to Mrs Kuperus, the headmistress of her first school – "we were both in tears as we said a heartbreaking farewell". At the lyceum Anne met Jacqueline van Maarsen and they soon became best friends, collecting and swapping postcards of film stars. In the summer of 1941, Edith's mother, the girls' dear Granny, became seriously ill and had to have an operation. She had lived with the family since 1939, when she had been persuaded to leave Germany for good. When she died in the winter of 1941-42, Anne wrote: "No one will ever know how much she is in my thoughts and how much I love her still."

◀ *Otto and Anne (second row, left-hand page) walk with other guests to a wedding on 16 July 1941. Anne's mother Edith stayed at home with Margot, who was ill.*

Anne receives the diary

At 6.00 a.m. on Friday, 12 June 1942, Anne woke up, full of excitement – it was her 13th birthday. She wasn't usually encouraged to get up so early, so she forced herself to stay in bed for another 45 minutes. At a quarter to seven she went into the family's dining room and played with Moortje, their cat. Then, unable to wait any longer, she went to find her parents and with them went to the living room to open her presents. Among the gifts was a red and white cloth-covered diary with a simple lock on the front, from her father. Anne was thrilled. Her first entry reads: "I hope I will be able to confide everything to you, as I have never been able to confide in anyone, and hope you will be a great source of comfort and support."

"Dearest Kitty"

Anne decided to personalize her diary as if she were confiding in her closest friend. She called the diary "Kitty" (after a character in a novel she liked) and usually started each entry with "Dearest Kitty". She stuck a photograph of herself on the inside cover and wrote: "Gorgeous photograph, isn't it!!!!"

Early diary entries were concerned with recording the events of her birthday and describing her school friends, their personalities and how they behaved. Like many girls of her age, she was very interested in boys. Hanneli (Lies) Goslar recalled: "Boys really liked her and she always liked it a lot when all the boys paid attention to her." Anne documented her opinions of all the boys in her class. She was a harsh critic, using descriptions such as "brat", "pest" and "obnoxious, two-faced, lying, snivelling little twit". Only one boy escaped unscathed. Anne said: "Harry Schap is the most decent boy in the class."

Hobbies and interests

Describing her hobbies and interests to "Kitty", "to lay the basis for our friendship", she wrote about the table tennis club she founded with four other girls. They called it "The Little Dipper, Minus Two", because they wanted a special name and thought the Little Dipper was made up of five stars. Later they discovered there were seven stars in this constellation, so they added the "Minus Two". The girls liked ice-cream, so after their matches they would cycle to the nearest ice-cream parlour that was allowed to serve Jews. They usually found boys who would buy them "more ice-cream than we could eat in a week".

In her diary Anne described her encounters with boys who wanted to cycle home with her and "were sure to fall for me on the spot". Often she would think up ruses to put the boys off. These included distraction and pretence. She might swerve her bike and let her satchel fall to the ground. While the boy stopped to pick it up, Anne had time to think of a way to steer the conversation. At other times, she would pretend to be insulted at something the boy said or did and insist that he went home without her.

"An incorrigible chatterbox"

Anne got on quite well with her teachers at the Jewish school. Mr Keesing, who taught maths, complained that she talked too much in class. After several warnings, he gave her some extra homework – to write an essay on being "A Chatterbox". Anne wrote three pages, arguing that talking is a female trait and that since her mother talked as much as she did, she had inherited this fault. She would do her best to control it, but might never be able

"to cure herself of the habit".

Mr Keesing had a tough job with Anne; no sooner was the essay handed in than Anne was chattering in class again. He set her another essay, the title of which was to be "An Incorrigible Chatterbox". After this Anne managed to be quiet for two whole lessons, but returned to chatting during the third. Finally, Keesing set her an essay entitled "Quack, Quack, said Mistress Chatterback". The whole class erupted in laughter as Anne was set the challenge of producing something original. Anne's friend Sanne, who was a budding poet, offered to help her write it in verse. Anne jumped at the chance of producing a clever piece of work and the poem was a great success when read aloud.

A few days after this classroom incident, Anne met a 16 year-old boy called Hello (Helmuth) Silberberg at a friend's house. He liked Anne and was soon cycling to school with her. Anne was flattered by his attentions, although she claimed to be in love with a boy called Peter Schiff, whom she had not seen for some time. When she saw Peter in the street while out with Helmuth, and he said hello to her, "it really made me feel good", she wrote. One evening Hello came over to Anne's house to visit. After a while they went for a walk and didn't get back to the Franks' house until ten minutes after the curfew time of 8.00 p.m. Anne's father was waiting anxiously for her return. He scolded her for her thoughtlessness and made her promise that in future she would be home before the curfew time, at ten minutes to eight. Later, Anne's mother teased her by asking whom she was going to marry. Anne's response was typically cheeky: "I bet she'll never guess it's Peter, because I talked her out of that idea myself."

A young girl's scrapbook

Anne stuck family snapshots into her diary, together with comments. Whenever she wanted to add anything, she would stick some loose sheets of paper inside. She also used two types of handwriting in the diary; printing and joined up writing. On 20 June 1942 she wrote: "It's an odd idea for someone like me to keep a diary; not only because I have never done so before, but because it seems to me that neither I – nor for that matter anyone else – will be interested in the unbosomings of a thirteen-year-old schoolgirl."

▶ *Anne's diary, a precious gift on her thirteenth birthday, became her special confidante.*

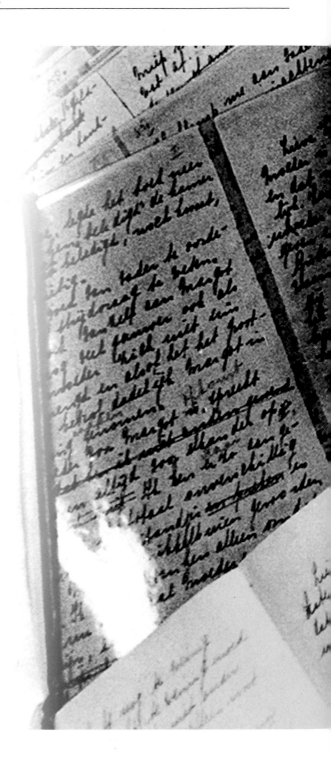

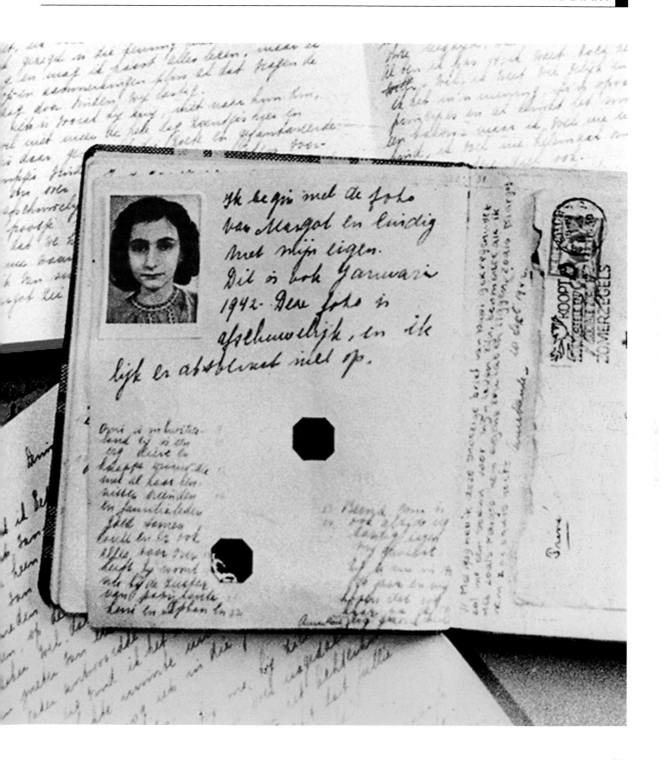

Going into hiding

Throughout 1941 Otto Frank began making arrangements to take his family into hiding. Otto's business had changed premises on 1 December 1940, moving to 263 Prinsengracht. It was here that Otto prepared a secret annexe, on the top two floors at the rear of the building.

In January 1942 the first "call-up" papers were served to Jews in Holland. At first only unemployed Jewish males were called upon to report for work in the eastern Netherlands. But soon whole families were summoned to go to Westerbork camp, formerly a transit camp for Jewish refugees seeking entry into Holland. From there the families were sent east to labour camps in overcrowded cattle cars, which had no heating, toilets or seating. Prisoners were given no food or water. The Jewish Council was pressured by the Nazis to deliver specific numbers of people to the camp at Westerbork. The quota was not met, so arrests were made at random by the Nazi special police force – the dreaded SS. Many Jews tried to find hiding places, mostly in the countryside, but only a small number were successful.

Otto Frank's plan

Because of the way in which events had unfolded in Germany, Otto Frank had anticipated the Nazis' anti-Jewish actions in Holland. In 1941 he had transferred the ownership of his business to two of his senior employees – Johannes (Jo) Kleiman and Victor Kugler – and the business name was changed from "Opekta – Works" to "Trading Company Gies & Co". Kugler and Kleiman, as well as Miep Gies and Elisabeth "Bep" Voskuijl, Otto's female office staff, were to become the Frank family's lifeline for two years.

While out walking with Anne one day, Otto told her something of his plans to take the family into hiding. On the morning of 5 July 1942 Anne chronicled in her diary his concern about living "cut

▶ *The deportation of Jewish families usually began at a railway station.*

▲ *Front and back views of the house at 263 Prinsengracht, Amsterdam, where Otto Frank's business was situated and where the Frank family would spend more than two years in hiding. The "Secret Annexe" is on the upper floors at the back.*

off from the world" and her own anxiety about this unexpected turn of events. During the afternoon the front doorbell rang at their home. It was a hot summer's day and Anne was sunbathing and reading outside on the flat roof. She didn't hear the bell, but a little later, a shaken Margot came up and told her that their father had received a "call-up" notice from the SS. This meant that he would be sent to a concentration camp and probably to his death. Later Margot admitted to Anne that the call-up paper wasn't for their father at all, but for her. Anne began to cry. She couldn't believe the Germans would transport a girl of 16 all by herself.

The plan becomes a reality

When Otto Frank returned home at 5.00 p.m, after visiting a friend, he discovered what had happened. During the afternoon Edith Frank had gone out and brought back Otto's business partner, Herman van Pels. The van Pels family – Herman, Auguste and their son Peter – would go into hiding with the Franks. Otto and Herman discussed final plans and then Herman left to fetch their friend Miep Gies.

Miep came and took away clothing, returning at 11.00 p.m. that night with her husband Jan to take more of the family's possessions to a secret hiding place. The next day, a warm wet Monday morning, Anne was woken up by her mother at 5.00 a.m. The whole family dressed in several layers of clothing. It would have been too suspicious for a Jewish family to be seen walking in the streets carrying suitcases so they wore whatever they could. Miep arrived to fetch Margot and they cycled off to their secret destination.

At 7.30 a.m. Anne and her parents left Merwedeplein forever. Anne was upset about leaving their cat Moortje behind, but they all wanted to reach a place of safety and at that moment nothing else mattered as much. As they trudged the five kilometres north through the rain to Prinsengracht, Anne was told the whole plan for going into hiding. She had not known that their refuge was to be inside her father's workplace or that so much thought and energy had gone into creating their sanctuary. The original plan was to go into hiding on 16 July, but the date had been brought forward because of Margot's sudden call-up.

The hiding place revealed

Miep Gies was waiting for the Franks when they arrived at 263 Prinsengracht. She led them along the corridor on the first floor and up the wooden stairs to the second floor where Margot was waiting. The annexe was at the back of the building on the top two floors. A small narrow hallway containing a steep flight of stairs and two doorways led to the first three rooms. The door to the right led to the bathroom – a windowless room with a basin and small lavatory cubicle. A door from this room gave access to the sisters' bedroom. The other door in the hall opened into the Frank family's living room and Otto and Edith's bedroom, with a communicating door into Anne and Margot's bedroom. The hall staircase led to the two rooms the van Pels family would occupy. The first was a large room containing a gas cooker and a sink, which was to be Mr and Mrs van Pels' bedroom as well as a living room, dining room and study for all the occupants. The second, a tiny side room, would serve as a bedroom for Peter van Pels. Above these two rooms, reached by a steep staircase in Peter's room was an attic, a quiet place where Anne would later go to write in her diary. A few weeks after their arrival Victor Kugler thought the entrance to their hiding place should be disguised. He asked Mr Voskuijl, Bep's father, to make a heavy, hinged bookcase that would swing open like a door.

Anne's annexe

In her diary Anne confided: "The annexe is an ideal place to hide in. It may be damp and lopsided, but there's probably not a more comfortable hiding place in all of Amsterdam. No, not in all of Holland." It took a lot of hard work to make the rooms habitable, but after a couple of days of cleaning and scrubbing some sort of order was established. Bep Voskuijl and Miep Gies went shopping with the Franks' ration coupons so that the family would have something to eat. Otto Frank had thought to bring Anne's postcard and film star collection to the annexe – he had even brought a pot of glue and a brush! Anne happily plastered the walls of her room with pictures and soon it looked more like home.

Edith and Margot were deeply affected by the move to the annexe and it took them a couple of days to recover from the experience. Anne and her father threw

▲ *A false bookcase concealed the staircase to the annexe, as revealed here by Otto's friend Johannes Kleiman.*

themselves into making black-out curtains for the apartment. Later, Anne wrote: "These works of art were tacked to the windows where they'll stay until we come out of hiding." Black-out curtains were essential to block out light and to protect against prying eyes.

Deportation of Dutch Jews started in the summer of 1942, during night raids. Jewish people were rounded up by police and transported in cattle trucks to

ons antwoord:
Het geweer
ter hand!

Gripland
Nijpland
Eng...nd

Vlamingen
alle in de ⚡⚡ Langemarck

▲ Tale of hatred: this wartime poster urges the
Langemarck Division of Hitler's SS to rid mainland
Europe of Jews before moving on to Great Britain.

Westerbork transit camp and from there to concentration camps in Poland (Auschwitz, Birkenau and Sobibor) and later to camps at Bergen-Belsen and Theresienstadt in Germany. Many tried to get exemption stamps in their ID papers or to obtain passports from other countries, but few were successful. Most escape routes were closed.

In the early years of the German occupation of Holland, the Dutch Resistance was not very effective. Religious and political differences hampered their organization. By 1942, however, they were helping to create false identity cards, find "hosts" who would take in Jews, and destroy registration offices where statistics helpful to the Nazis were kept.

By late 1944 about a quarter of a million non-Jewish Dutch were in hiding, while another 900,000 had left their homes to evade deportation to Germany as forced labour. Of the 24,000 Jews in hiding during the war, 16,000 survived, while 8,000 were discovered and then killed.

A typical teenager

Anne was a typically volatile young girl, and in the confined atmosphere of the Secret Annexe her feelings were sometimes exaggerated, even confused.

Anne felt that her mother got on better with Margot than with her, which was true to some extent as Edith Frank and Margot were much more in sympathy with one another. Margot was a quiet and studious 16-year-old, who was more of a companion to their mother. Anne wrote: "They're so sentimental together, but I'd rather be sentimental on my own." Anne adored her father, who was fondly nicknamed "Pim" by his daughters. She felt that he was the only one who really understood her. She often felt aggrieved, though, when Pim sided with Edith and Margot over some argument with Anne. She also hated the way in which her mother talked about her to people she described as "outsiders" (for example, Mr and Mrs van Pels). In reality, Anne's mother probably found the situation – being confined with a difficult teenage daughter – very wearing and needed someone to talk to about it. For her part Anne was spirited and independent-minded, often clashing with her mother in the way that many teenage girls do.

A teenager in hiding

After one particularly heated argument, over a book Margot was reading and she wanted, Anne let rip in her diary about her feelings for her mother and sister. She wrote that she loved them, but only because they were mother and Margot, and she didn't give a "dash" for them as people. She went on to say that she clung to her father because of the contempt that she felt for her mother. Towards the end of this diary entry, full of normal teenage self-righteousness, Anne says, "The worst part is that father and mother don't realize their own inadequacies and how much I blame them for letting me down. Are there any parents who can make their children completely happy?"

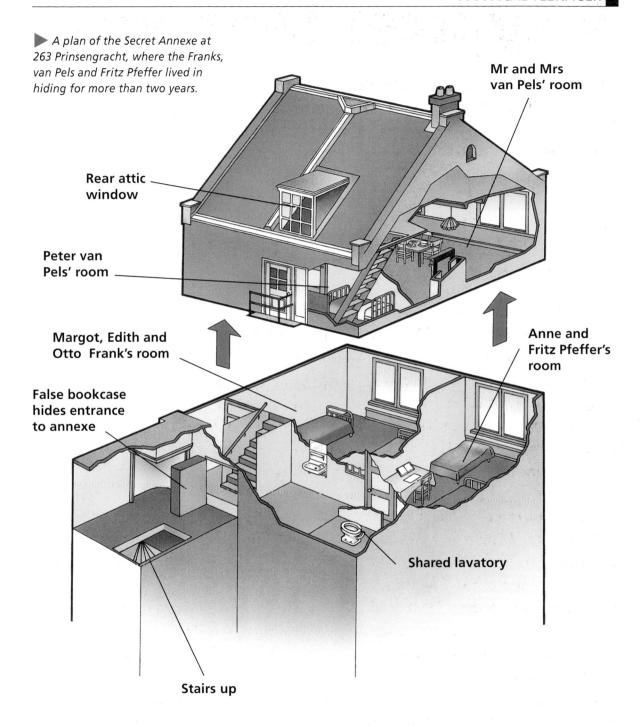

A plan of the Secret Annexe at 263 Prinsengracht, where the Franks, van Pels and Fritz Pfeffer lived in hiding for more than two years.

Mr and Mrs van Pels' room

Rear attic window

Peter van Pels' room

Margot, Edith and Otto Frank's room

False bookcase hides entrance to annexe

Anne and Fritz Pfeffer's room

Shared lavatory

Stairs up

Anne's rebelliousness was no doubt fuelled by the frustration of her virtual imprisonment in the annexe and the fact that she felt the loss of her friends keenly. In the absence of friends, school and freedom, her imaginary friend Kitty became the outlet for her emotions.

The van Pels arrive

The van Pels (called the van Daans in Anne's diary) joined the Frank family in hiding on 13 July 1942. They should have arrived on the 14th, but from 13-16 July the Germans had been issuing mass call-up notices, so Mr and Mrs van Pels had decided to err on the side of caution and go into hiding as soon as possible. Anne's life became more interesting after the van Pels family moved in. It had been too quiet for her before, with no other focus but her immediate family; this had made her nervous and prone to bouts of tears. Peter van Pels was the first of the family to arrive at the annexe as the Franks were having breakfast. Anne's first impression of him was that he was a shy, awkward 16-year-old boy "whose company won't amount to much". Herman and Auguste

◀ *Auguste (left) and Herman van Pels, who shared the annexe with the Franks.*

van Pels arrived half an hour later. Part of Mrs van Pels' luggage was a hatbox containing a large chamber pot. This greatly amused Anne and her parents.

While the Franks found the van Pels amusing in small ways, in her diary Anne said of them, "some people seem to take special delight not only in raising their own children but in helping others to raise theirs". Now Anne felt that she was being scolded by four adults, two of whom were not even her own parents. Most of the time her mother and father would spring to her defence over some criticism – usually levelled by Mrs van Pels – and Anne later confessed that without her parents' support she wouldn't have been able to cope so well with these scoldings. When a squabble developed over Anne's eating habits during one mealtime, Otto Frank retorted, "look who's calling the kettle black!". This silenced Auguste van Pels, who wouldn't eat beans or cabbage for dinner because she said they gave her wind. Anne was amused when Mrs van Pels blushed with embarrassment, as she so easily did.

From the start the two families ate their meals together and after three days Anne said it felt as if the seven of them had become one big family. Mr van Pels filled them in on what had happened when they'd left their flat. Edith Frank had left a note with a Maastricht address on it so that neighbours, friends and anyone else who enquired would think that they had gone there en route to Belgium and Switzerland. Mr van Pels reported that he had heard from several people that this was where the Franks had gone, so the trick had worked.

Room for one more

Tragic reports of what was happening to the Jews were getting more frequent by the day. Their friends in the office, who kept them informed, knew of a Dutch Jew who needed to find a "safe house" and they asked the Franks and van Pels if they would consider harbouring one more fugitive. The two families agreed that eight could eat as well as seven and there was just enough room for another person in their hiding place. So Miep's dentist, a man named Fritz Pfeffer, was the last person to join them. Otto also knew Pfeffer and was keen to help him.

Fritz Pfeffer was a 53-year-old man who had been living with a Christian woman several years younger than himself. He was reported to be good with children, quiet and refined. Miep conducted the negotiations and tried to get him to come to the hiding place at Prinsengracht as soon as possible. Although Pfeffer could not come immediately, he was relieved to have found a hiding place and turned up at the annexe several days later.

The arrival of Fritz Pfeffer signalled a reorganization of the annexe. He was to share Anne's bedroom, while Margot moved in with her parents. At first, Anne thought Mr Pfeffer was a nice man, who was agreeable to sharing a room with her. She wasn't delighted at having someone she didn't know using her things, but she was prepared to make sacrifices for a good cause. With the impatience of youth, she was surprised that Pfeffer was so slow to catch on to the way in which things were done in the annexe. She wrote, "he asks everything twice and still can't remember what you've told him".

Anne soon revised her opinion of Mr Pfeffer as he turned out to be "an old-fashioned disciplinarian and preacher of unbearably long sermons on manners".

▶ *Fritz Pfeffer was a middle-aged dentist, who was unused to sharing his space with strangers, least of all a lively teenage girl.*

She felt that he made a bad situation worse by criticizing her in the same way as the others, and he reported her apparent faults and misdeeds to her mother. Anne was getting more and more fed up with everyone criticizing and complaining about her and she confided to her diary on more than one occasion about the unfairness of the situation.

Too close for comfort

Life in the annexe was hard on all the occupants. They lived in cramped conditions with almost no privacy, no fresh air and a daily eight-hour ban on talking. After a while each person's little ways and habits became extremely annoying to the others and disputes over "territory" became more frequent.

By 22 December 1942 Anne wrote that she was always being scolded for making too much noise. Everyone kept saying "shh" to her, and Mr Pfeffer had taken to "shhing" her in the night, when she so much as coughed or turned over!

Anne found one of Pfeffer's habits particularly aggravating. This was his Sunday morning exercise session at the crack of dawn. He would "lumber" about in the little room they shared, bumping into chairs as he dressed and making it impossible for her to sleep. In her diary entry of 28 November 1942 Anne complained about sharing "my far too narrow room with His Excellency …" She may have been a typical teenager, but these were exceptional circumstances.

Not surprisingly, Anne was disturbed by nightmares at this time, probably brought on by Pfeffer's tales of what was happening on the streets of Amsterdam.

Happy Hanukkah!

In December 1942 Hanukkah (the Jewish festival of light) and St Nicholas' Day almost coincided. For Hanukkah, candles were lit in the annexe and gifts exchanged, as was the custom. According to Anne, St Nicholas' Day was more fun, with surprise gifts for everyone, including their "protectors" downstairs.

The following year Anne hatched a plan with her father to cheer everyone up. At a quarter to eight in the evening they brought in a basket, which had been decorated with paper cutouts and bows. On top was a poem: "Let's not forget it's St Nicholas' Day, though we've nothing left to give away". The basket contained a shoe belonging to each person, with a small gift tucked inside. This gesture was typical of Anne's often warm-hearted nature.

Razias (night raids) by the Gestapo on Jewish homes were becoming more frequent and while the hideaways tried not to dwell on these events during the day, at night it was sometimes impossible to stop thinking about them. Sometimes Anne awoke in the middle of the night and cried out, disturbing the others and needing comfort and reassurance before she could go back to sleep. On these occasions, it was usually Anne's father who went to her, even though her mother was willing to do so and was always protective of her two daughters.

▼ *A view of the room in the Secret Annexe that Anne shared with Fritz Pfeffer, as it is today.*

Daily life in the annexe

For Anne, one of the worst aspects of living in the annexe was the effort of staying quiet throughout the day. No one could suspect that they occupied a part of the Prinsengracht business premises and therefore silence was essential during business hours.

It must have been very hard for the eight people waiting with bated breath. They dared not exercise, wash or flush the toilet during the working part of the day, although they could read, write, study and play games. From Monday to Friday the office hours at Trading Company Gies and Co were 8.30 a.m. to 5.30 p.m. with an hour or so for lunch. During this break the residents of the annexe gathered to eat, listen to the BBC's 1.00 p.m. radio broadcast and do any washing or cleaning that was necessary before they resumed their rule of silence until the end of the working day. In early August 1943 Anne documented their daily activities in detail in her diary. She made light of these daily events, but in reality life in the annexe was not fun. Right from the start the occupants of the annexe made themselves useful. They pitted fruit for preserves, filled packets with gravy powder and did simple office work to relieve those downstairs of some of their workload. They also had to store and prepare their own food, which was obtained using black market ration books, paid for with the two families' savings. They bought 140 kg of beans and stored them in the attic.

One of the sacks burst while it was being carried up the stairs, sending a shower of beans cascading down on Anne. Mr van Pels showed a talent for making

▶ *Food was in desperately short supply in Amsterdam during the war years. This picture shows people queuing outside a shop.*

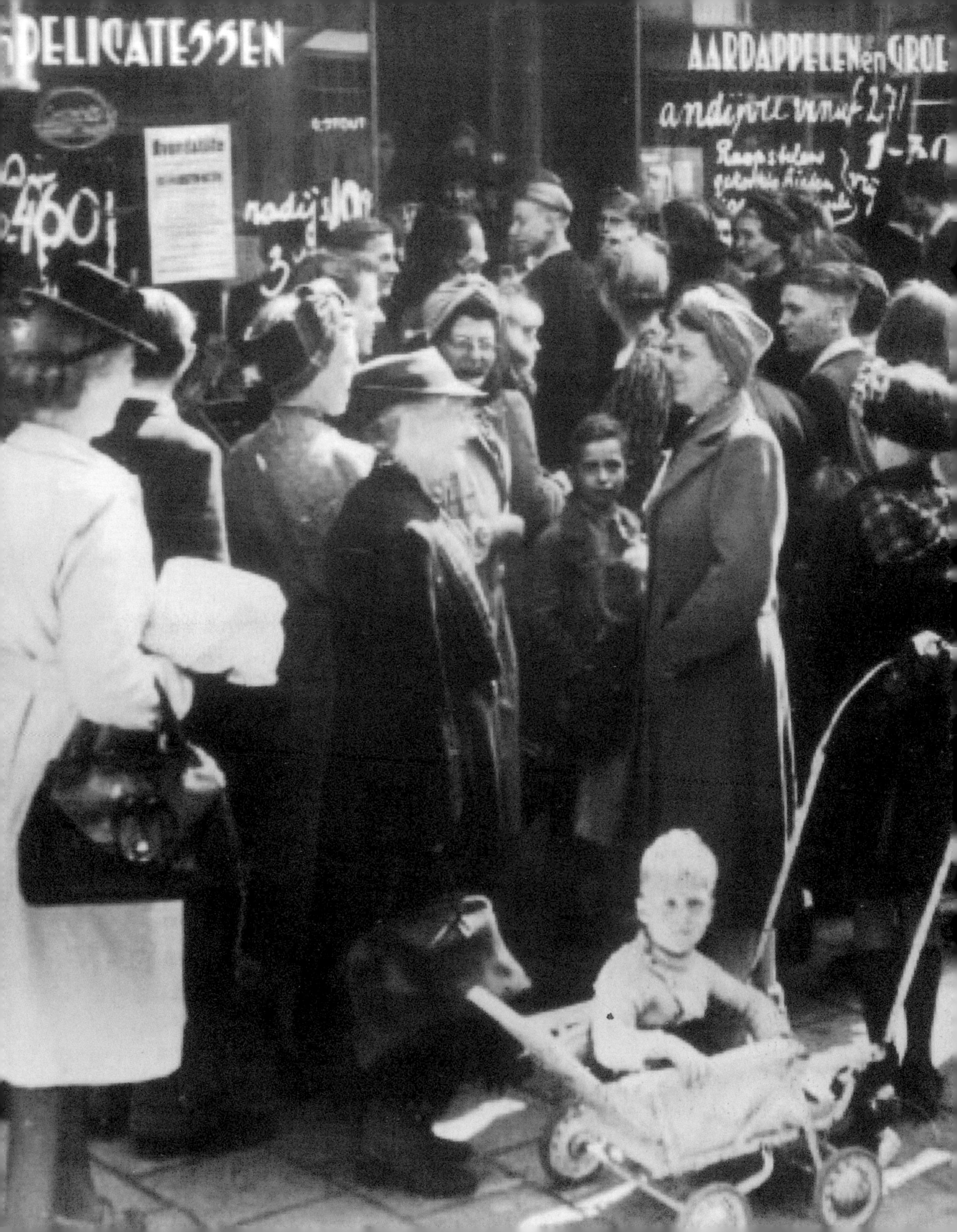
DELICATESSEN
AARDAPPELEN en GROE

sausage and produced bratwurst and mettwurst sausages from the meat they bought on the black market. He made the sausages and strung them on a pole suspended from the ceiling. Everyone laughed at the sight of the curing sausages as they dangled comically overhead.

Human habits

"The strangest things happen when you're in hiding," Anne would write on 29 September 1942, regarding the bathing habits of the members of the two families. All they had to wash in was a galvanized tin tub and each person chose a different place in the building to wash. When it was their turn to have a bath they would take the tub to their preferred spot and carry out their ablutions in the privacy of their chosen surroundings. Everyone had a specific time to use the washing facilities, although less rigid rules applied to the use of the lavatory. With a touch of characteristic humour, Anne recounted Fritz Pfeffer's toilet routine and the urgent needs of the people kept waiting by him. She wrote, "He never

◀ *Anne spent much time looking out of the small attic window of the Secret Annexe, shown in this side view of 263 Prinsengracht.*

deviates or lets himself be swayed by the voices outside the door, begging him to open up before a disaster occurs."

While they had to remain in hiding, they didn't neglect their studies or reading. Mr Kleiman brought books to the annexe every week and always picked out two especially for Anne: "written for girls my age". Their friends in the office also organized a correspondence course in shorthand for those who were interested, and English, French and Dutch were taught by occupants of the annexe who had become reasonably fluent in these languages. Anne continued with her schoolwork too, and was progressing well with her Dutch. Every day, between the hours of 2.30–4.00 p.m., she used the table in her own (and Fritz Pfeffer's) bedroom for studying. She asked Pfeffer if she could extend her use of the table until 5.30 two afternoons a week. When he refused, Anne called in her father as mediator and Pfeffer reluctantly gave in. But in the way of many such petty squabbles, Pfeffer reacted by not speaking to Anne for two days.

To keep fit all the inhabitants of the annexe took part in an evening session of calisthenics – a form of exercise that could be done in a small space, and which promoted suppleness and muscular strength. Sometimes the inhabitants of the annexe would sing or even dance, but only after 6.00 p.m., when the workers had gone home, and then only very softly. In her diary, Anne made a note of her favourite hobbies. Top of the list was writing, including made-up stories, then genealogy (she spent hours researching the family trees of European royal families), next came history and mythology and last but not least pictures of film stars and family, many of which were found in her papers. The group also played games, which they had brought with them to pass the time. Sometimes they told jokes and riddles and reviewed books they had read.

Anne also discovered the dubious joys of voyeurism – she used a pair of binoculars at night to stare into the lit windows opposite. She commented: "I never knew that neighbours could be so interesting. Ours are, at any rate. I've come across a few at dinner, one family making a cine film and the dentist opposite working on a frightened old lady."

A radio lifeline

Apart from their helpers, the only contact they had with the outside world was through their radio. In Otto Frank's old office there was a large Philips wireless. They would all gather around this in the evenings when the office staff had gone home and experience a sort of freedom granted by

the airwaves. The annexe rules were that they could only listen to the radio after 6.00 p.m., and not to German broadcasts (especially German news bulletins) unless they were classical

▶ *Anne decorated the wall of her room with pictures of movie stars and celebrities.*

KOM OOK
IN DEN GERMAANSCHEN
LANDDIENST
IN HET OOSTEN

music programmes. By June 1943 the German authorities demanded that all private radios must be handed over. This was because the messages people were receiving indicated that the Germans were starting to lose the war. All over Holland people were trying to get hold of old radios, which they could hand in to the authorities in place of their own "morale boosters". Jo Kleiman had hidden a small radio set in his house and gave this to the members of the annexe when the office radio had to be handed in at the end of July.

An appointment with the annexe dentist

An old-fashioned foot-driven dentist's drill was found for Fritz Pfeffer. His first patient at the annexe practice was Mrs van Pels, who had two teeth that needed attention. When he started to scrape out the cavity in one of her teeth, he struck a nerve, making her jump out of the chair with the probe still embedded in the tooth. Eventually, with Anne and Mr van Pels holding her down in the chair, Mr Pfeffer finished the job. Anne was not impressed. "The whole scene resembled one of those engravings from the Middle Ages entitled 'A Quack at Work'."

◀ *This poster urges Dutch people to collaborate with the Nazis by joining the "Landdienst", a labour service, to work on farms in the east and help the Nazi war effort.*

Constant fear

Even at night their troubles could not be easily forgotten. Air raids and anti-aircraft gunfire often woke them from whatever rest they could get. Anne and Mrs van Pels were particularly affected by the noises. Anne would crawl into her father's bed, shaking with nerves, only to return to her own bed when the "all clear" sounded. On a particularly bad day the RAF made three raids on Amsterdam. As the bombs rained down, the Prinsengracht house shook and Anne clung tightly to her "escape bag", which contained all the things she would need if she and her family were forced to evacuate their hiding place in a hurry.

Heroic helpers

The majority of the Dutch population resented the German occupation of their country, although at first few did anything to oppose Nazi rule. Many people felt there was no middle ground and they had to make a choice between Fascism and Communism.

Most Dutch people's religious principles, coupled with their country's history, would not allow them to opt for a godless political system such as Communism. However, by the autumn of 1942 the German setbacks in Russia and North Africa and the end of Mussolini's regime in Italy encouraged those who wished to resist the Nazis.

Although some Dutch collaborators helped the Germans, they experienced passive as well as active resistance from many other Dutch citizens. The biggest contributor to the German war effort in the Netherlands was the NSB, the Dutch National Socialist (Nazi) organization. On an individual level, profit rather than political belief often supplied the motive for collaboration. Recruits from the Dutch male population were sought to fight on the German "Eastern Front" in Russia. In 1940–41 30,000 men and boys volunteered, and in April 1941 17,000 entered service with the Waffen SS, the military arm of the SS. Many others worked in supporting roles, helping to supply the troops, build roads or military installations, or act as police or guards in prisoner of war and concentration camps.

In 1943 vital records regarding population statistics were destroyed when Amsterdam's registration office was set on fire by a Resistance group. Files of records from other towns' registration offices also disappeared and were hidden away so that the Germans could not make use of the information they contained. Anne wrote in her diary about the Amsterdam fire, "One good piece of news is that the Labour Exchange was set on fire in an act of sabotage. A few days later the Register

▶ *Anton Mussert was the leader of the Dutch Nazi movement. Here he meets Hitler's hated and feared deputy, Heinrich Himmler (left), on 26 May 1942.*

◀ *Miep Gies and Bep Voskuijl in 1945.*

Office also went up in flames. Men posing as German police bound and gagged the guards and managed to destroy some important documents."

No place to hide

Thousands of Jews tried to hide from their German persecutors, but very few succeeded. The most important factor in the success or failure of dropping out of sight was obtaining reliable help. But finding somebody who was willing to help was only the first obstacle to be overcome. Sometimes the Resistance would find a "host" who would shelter a fugitive. However, the fugitive was taking an enormous risk, as their "host" would have no personal feelings of loyalty to sustain them over a long and stressful period of time.

Some Jews found themselves exploited by their hosts, who in effect blackmailed them (for jewellery and money) and then sometimes went on to denounce them to the authorities. The Franks and their fellow hideaways were very fortunate in their four helpers. These good people were Otto's office staff, whom he had known and trusted for many years. He had even signed over his businesses to two of them (Kleiman and Kugler) for the duration of the war. He was especially friendly with Miep Gies and her husband Jan (a member of the Dutch Resistance), but each one of the helpers was encouraged by their own beliefs and sense of justice to help their friends, which is how they regarded the hideaways.

Anne wrote about their "protectors", the heroic people who helped them, but she only saw "the tip of the iceberg". There are many peripheral characters in her diary, such as the grocer who delivered the potatoes to the office every lunchtime. She didn't know that he was also involved with a Resistance group, and that he and his wife gave refuge to two Jewish men in their apartment until they were betrayed in 1944.

Obtaining food

In Otto's memoir he mentions the role of each of the "helpers". The two women, Miep and Bep, provided the food for all eight of the inhabitants of the annexe. Jo Kleiman and Miep's husband, Jan Gies, obtained black market (illegal because they violated the restrictions on goods) ration cards for the residents and also arranged the sale of jewellery when their money ran low. Mr Kleiman had a friend who ran a bakery chain in Amsterdam. He arranged to have bread delivered twice a week to the office, part of the cost of which was paid on delivery of the bread. The balance was to be charged to account and paid for when the war was over. Obtaining food and supplies was not an easy task. Many hours were spent queuing for groceries with no guarantee that any food would be left by the time the counter was reached. The rationing of butter and cooking fat was particularly severe and sometimes none at all could be obtained. Bep was also responsible for the supply of milk and fresh fruit to the annexe. Fruit was expensive and could only be obtained when prices were low. Since almost everything was bought on the black market, staying in hiding was expensive. Mies sometimes managed to get meat from a butcher friend of Mr van Pels, who had taken her to the shop before he went into hiding. To help out with the hideaways' finances, Victor Kugler sold spices without keeping traceable records. This money went towards the hideaways' provisions.

Keeping up the spirits

Apart from foodstuffs, clothes and medicines, the helpers also provided books, moral support and news from the outside world. Miep, Jan and Bep would occasionally stay the night in the annexe and this would raise everyone's spirits, giving some semblance of normality. At midday too, when the other workers had left the building, one or two of the helpers might have lunch in the annexe. Later, Miep remembered a night she spent there: "The quietness of the place was overwhelming. The fright of these people who were locked up here was so thick I could feel it pressing down on me. It was like a thread of terror pulled taut. It was so terrible it never let me close my eyes."

Carrying on "normally" became a

Breaking the law to shelter a Jew

It was an illegal act to shelter a Jew from the authorities; any helper had to be ready to face extreme and arbitrary punishment if caught. The penalties for defying the law could range from temporary imprisonment and torture to death in a concentration camp. These helpers were truly heroic souls, since nobody knew how long the war might last, or even if the Nazis would lose it.

calculated risk as everything a helper did had to be weighed up against the likelihood of discovery by another "law-abiding" citizen.

It was important that the helpers felt that they would be able to hold out against the odds and be successful in saving their friends' lives. The survival of those in hiding depended on them, which was a great and sometimes terrible responsibility. Miep, who felt morally bound to keep her friends safe, "never felt any desire to be free of the Frank family". She sensed their dependence keenly, with the exception of Anne who was nearly always bright and cheerful, greeting her friends with a barrage of questions and tales of life in the annexe.

A loyal network

Anne's helpers were lucky in one way in that they shared the burden with each other and most had the support of their own families. Miep had her husband Jan, Bep was helped by her father, Johan Voskuijl (who made the bookcase for the annexe), Jo Kleiman had the support of his wife; only Victor Kugler kept his involvement a secret.

By the autumn of 1944 things were

Miep Gies, a true friend

Born Hermine Santrouschitz in Vienna in 1909, Miep was sent to Holland in 1920 at the age of 11 as part of a programme for undernourished children. She grew up there, with foster parents, and never returned to Austria. She started working for Otto Frank in 1933. As Hitler rose to power in Germany and Nazism took hold, Miep, a Christian, became increasingly alarmed and appalled at the persecution of minority groups, especially Jews. She shared these views with Otto and often discussed politics with him. When Germany invaded Holland and the Frank family were put in immediate danger, Miep didn't hesitate to offer them help. In 1941 she married Jan Gies and became a Dutch citizen.

much worse for the Dutch population as a whole. German repression in Holland increased as the Nazis lost the initiative elsewhere in Europe and took out their frustration on the occupied Dutch. However, about 30,000 people were actively involved in resisting the Germans by listening to forbidden Allied radio broadcasts and distributing information through the then-established underground press.

At the beginning of the war no organizations existed in the Netherlands to help fugitives "go underground". For most Jews it was a question of finding Christian friends or acquaintances who were willing to help them, as with the Franks. It was unusual for a family to be able to hide together in one place. Often, children were brought to a sympathetic friend, who would take them in or find a "safe address" for them. Several thousand Jewish children were saved in this way, many finding homes with farmers in the countryside. Few saw their parents again. When a friend's grandchildren were brought to their house one night, Miep and Jan managed to find a student organization in Amsterdam that held a list of safe addresses where children could be brought. As the war went on, Jan became involved with the Dutch Resistance and, through his contacts, was able to obtain ration tickets, books and magazines for his friends in the Secret Annexe. When the Allies liberated Holland in April 1945, over 75 per cent of the Jewish population – more than 100,000 people – had been killed.

▶ *An unusual overhead view of a model of the room that Anne shared with Fritz Pfeffer, giving some idea of the crowded conditions in the Secret Annexe.*

Growing pains

On 12 February 1944, Anne wrote in her diary: "I think spring is inside me. I feel it in my entire body and soul . . . I only know that I'm longing for something." With these words Anne summed up her feelings of sexual awakening.

By the beginning of 1944, the occupants of the annexe had been in hiding for 18 months. Anne was growing up quickly and while still quick-tempered, she was becoming more reflective and sympathetic. She and Peter van Pels were opposites, but naturally enough in the circumstances they became attracted to each other. He was quiet and self-conscious, and he admired Anne for the way in which she expressed herself and seemed never to be lost for words. They were experiencing some of the same frustrations – being cooped up and unable to express themselves – and they found that they could talk to each other about their feelings. Peter's increasing fascination with Anne seemed to come at just the right time for her. She was lonely and missing her friends and she desperately needed to be appreciated. In

her diary, she wrote: "I sensed a strong feeling of fellowship, which I only remember having had with my girlfriends." Soon Anne and Peter were spending more and more time together.

Hopes for the future

As Anne and Peter talked – about all sorts of things – their relationship began to develop. Sometimes, they would sit in the attic, looking at the sky, the trees and birds and feel so close and so happy that words were not necessary. At other times they discussed the past, present and future and what they might do when the war was over. Peter wanted to find work on a rubber plantation in the Dutch East

▶ *At 13 Anne was a vivacious, intelligent girl. She never considered herself to be as beautiful or clever as Margot, but those around her were aware of her charm.*

Peter van Pels

Born on 8 November 1926 in Osnabruck, Peter had thick brown hair and blue eyes. Friends and relatives described him as shy and self-conscious, but with a sweet nature. In spite of Anne's initial, rather dismissive view of him, Peter's character often struck a chord with her. Like Anne, he loved the theatre and dressing up. On one occasion, to entertain their families, Peter put on one of his mother's very tight dresses and a hat, while Anne donned a suit and cap. "The grown-ups were doubled up with laughter." Anne also warmed to Peter because of his fondness for his cat Mouschi. Anne later described Peter as "honest and generous, modest and helpful."

Indies. He told Anne that he wouldn't want anyone to know that he was Jewish, a comment that disappointed her because she had such a strong sense of her identity. Annc had decided she would become a Dutch citizen and work as a journalist "and later on a famous writer". She was an avid reader and a good student. And as well as keeping up with her diary, she had started to write stories.

Still at odds with her mother, Anne felt

◀ *Peter van Pels was not talkative like Anne, but he was practical and good with his hands. He enjoyed carpentry and other chores.*

a common bond with Peter, whose own mother – she felt – was a shallow woman. Anne also sympathized with Peter because he was not at ease with himself ("Little does he know it's his awkwardness I find so touching.") and she knew that his parents often argued, which upset him. She started to write in her diary about love: "Love is understanding someone, caring for him, sharing his joys and sorrows. This eventually includes physical love."

Introspection and emotions

At this time, Anne had vivid dreams about her first "crush", Peter Schiff, whom she hardly knew. In real life the dream Peter and the real Peter merged into an ideal person whom Anne could love. As she began to examine her feelings for Peter van Pels, she became more analytical, and more critical, both of herself and those close to her. People had always told her that she was attractive, generous and funny, but now she wondered if she was over-confident and conceited, merely "a terrible flirt, coquettish and amusing". In one touching entry in her diary (7 March 1944) she wrote about how the changes in her life had affected her and how she had been struggling to come to terms with her own shortcomings. Anne also experienced some feelings of jealousy in relation to Peter. She was convinced that Margot harboured feelings for him as well and this made her unhappy. When Margot gave Anne a letter in which she explained that she was fond of Peter, but the fondness was that of a sister for a brother, Anne was relieved. She confided to her diary about her longing for a boyfriend, her love for Peter, and about beauty and happiness. "A person who's happy will make others happy; a person who has courage and faith will never die in misery!"

A red letter day

Anne's fondness for Peter mirrored – and to some extent replaced – her affection for her father. In one diary entry she wrote: "Peter's a terrific chap, just like father". On 15 April 1944 ("…a red letter day for me"), Peter kissed Anne for the first time, sparking off mutual feelings of excitement and pleasure. This may have been an adolescent love, but for these two young people, cut off from the world, it was their first and only experience of being in love. They found comfort in hugging and kissing and simply lying cradled in each other's arms. Anne told her diary: "Why should we wait until we've reached a suitable age? Why should we ask anybody's permission?"

Despite this defiance, Anne felt that she must, in all honesty, tell her parents about the growing relationship. Part of her probably wanted to share these exciting new feelings with someone too. In the end it was, of course, her father she decided to confide in. She found a quiet moment in which to tell him that she and Peter had become close and although they were just friends, their relationship could develop into something deeper. Otto was as understanding as he saw fit, but he warned his daughter not to get too intense – a danger when the two young people spent so much time in each other's company. He told Anne that she must be the responsible one because, although he liked Peter, he felt he was immature and easily influenced. Anne respected her father and listened to what he had to say, but she was very much a free spirit and she wouldn't stop going to the attic to be with Peter, as her father wished.

A growing independence

Soon after their conversation, Anne wrote her father a letter, in which she told him that she had fought hard to become an independent person, with no help from anyone, and now that she had succeeded she didn't need to account to her parents for her actions. The next day Anne and her father had a long talk, during which she realized how hurtful her letter had been to him. Full of remorse, she wrote later: "This is the worst thing I've ever done in my life. Anyone who deliberately causes such pain to someone they say they love is despicable, the lowest of the low." Anne was ashamed that she'd hurt her father. She determined to learn from this experience, be less self-righteous and more forgiving. With Peter's help, she felt she could develop a good character, be someone those she cared about would be proud of. "I'll take father as my example once again, and I will improve myself."

Even though things settled down after this, a couple of months later Anne confided to her diary: "No one understands me!" She and Peter continued to be close, but in Anne's view their relationship wasn't progressing and

Growing girls

Otto and Edith Frank kept a record of their two daughters' heights on the bedroom wall. The marks are still there today, at the Anne Frank house, and show that Anne grew more than 13 centimetres in two years. Before long, the clothes they had brought with them to the annexe became too small and had to be altered. Occasionally Miep would bring the girls a new item of clothing, but most of the time they had to make do. On 2 May 1943 Anne noted that her vests were "so small that they don't even come to my tummy".

she found this frustrating. She was impatient, wishing that Peter could be less reserved and more communicative.

Anne had changed from the schoolgirl who had first come to live in the annexe, lively and bright but often quarrelsome. She had been growing up in the most difficult circumstances and now spent more time thinking about all sorts of things, trying to make sense of the world she lived in. In one of the last entries in Anne's diary, she wrestles with the question that women were thought to be inferior to men and the injustice of this notion. At just 15 years of age, Anne was showing true depth of character and a wisdom beyond her years.

The outside world

During the two years that Anne and her family were in hiding, many events took place in the world that would end the war and shape the future of the rest of the twentieth century.

Anne was only aware of these events through radio broadcasts, news from the helpers and what little she could hear and see at night, peering round the edge of the black-out curtains that covered the office windows.

The "Final Solution"

In December, 1941 the Nazis, in their tyranny over the German nation, commenced *Endlösung*, the "Final Solution". This was a plan to carry out the systematic mass murder of European Jews. They based their plans on their previous partial extermination of disabled people in Germany in the late 1930s, in an attempt to "purify" the German race. On 20 January 1942 the Wannsee Conference was held near Berlin, chaired

▶ As the Franks hid in Amsterdam, elsewhere the fate of thousands of European Jews was being decided. Here, Jewish people in Würzburg, Germany, are marched off to concentration camps.

by Adolf Eichmann. This meeting put the finishing touches to the plan and "rubber stamped" the proposed deaths of 11 million Jewish people. Unknown numbers of "undesirable groups" were also to be killed in this purge, including political opponents, so called "anti-social elements", Jehovah's Witnesses, Russian prisoners of war and hundreds of thousands of gypsies.

Transportation of Jews

Miep told the occupants of the annexe about the mass round-ups of Jews during October 1942. She described the horrors of the transportation of people in cattle trucks to Westerbork, the large transit camp which many Jews had been through on their way into Holland from Germany. The Gestapo treated their Jewish prisoners with great cruelty, shaving their heads to distinguish them from Christians. Bep told them about the young men who were sent to Germany to work in the factories there. They also heard that the Germans would take hostages against any damage caused to buildings or transport useful to the

◀ *Suffering and despair is evident on the faces of this Jewish family in Warsaw, 1943.*

German military. Punishment for this offence was the execution of five innocent hostages if the Gestapo couldn't find the saboteurs responsible. Anne was appalled and wrote: "Fine specimens of humanity, those Germans and to think I'm actually one of them! No, that's not true, Hitler took away our nationality long ago."

News of the war elsewhere

The radio gave those in the annexe important news of what was happening outside Holland, in the theatre of war. In November 1942 they heard that the Russian city of Stalingrad had still not fallen to the Germans and that the British had started to win battles against the German army in North Africa. When they heard that the British had landed in Oran, Tunis, Algiers and Casablanca, and all but Tunis were in British hands, morale inside the annexe began to improve greatly.

When Fritz Pfeffer had joined them he told them what was happening to the Jews "on the streets". He described the green and grey army vehicles that drove up and down, taking away Jewish families. It was impossible to escape them, he said, unless you went into hiding. It seemed that the Germans already had lists of Jewish names, stating who lived where. Sometimes they would offer a bounty for each Jew captured. The round-ups usually happened at night and Jews captured in Amsterdam were taken and held in the Jewish Theatre before going on to Westerbork camp. From there they were usually transported to the infamous camps of Auschwitz-Birkenau and Sobibor in Poland.

The suffering of the Dutch

Sometimes Anne sat downstairs in the front office after dark and peeped through a gap between the heavy black-out curtains. From her vantage point she could see what went on in the streets. How she must have longed for a taste of freedom, just to be able to breathe fresh air and walk along the canal. She wrote about the neighbourhood in which they were hiding, about the dirty little children with runny noses who played outside. Later, she wrote in her diary that things were so bad in war-torn Holland that the children ran around in thin shirts and wooden clogs: "They have no coats, no socks, no caps and no one to

help them." Food and fuel were in short supply and many children were cold, miserable and hungry.

From her window Anne observed that people seemed to be in a tearing hurry. Bicycles whizzed past so quickly that she couldn't see who was on them. One evening she saw two Jews walking by. This sight was so unusual that she wrote, "I felt as though I were looking at one of the Seven Wonders of the World. It gave me such a funny feeling, as if I'd denounced them to the authorities and was now spying on their misfortune."

Anne also wrote about the tragedy of people who returned home to find their houses boarded up and their families gone. These Jews would have been taken away before making their long and possibly last journey to a concentration camp in Germany.

Allied bombers overhead

Almost every night Allied bombers roared overhead on their way to destroy the cities and industries of Germany. Apart from hearing the planes going over, the radio broadcasts also informed them

▶ *By 1943, Allied bombers were destroying German cities in huge raids. This is part of Hamburg.*

of the terrible damage and carnage on both sides. Thousands of tons of high explosive rained down night after night on the industrial centres and cities of western Germany, causing many casualties. Amsterdam was bombed several times and, on one memorable occasion, three times in one day.

On 19 July 1943 Anne wrote about one particularly damaging raid, which had taken place the day before, when North Amsterdam was targeted. Whole streets were destroyed and children were reported to be searching in the ruins for their parents. The initial death toll was 200 with many more people injured.

The fall of Mussolini

One of the best pieces of news that Anne and her family received was of the fall of Benito Mussolini, the fascist dictator of Italy. On 26 July 1943 Mussolini resigned and King Victor Emmanuel III of Italy took over the government of the country. By the beginning of August the Fascist Party had been banned and on 8 September the inhabitants of the Secret Annexe heard on their radio that Italy had unconditionally surrendered. The surrender had been agreed on

3 September, the day the British landed in Naples. In October the Allies broke through German defence lines and in November they seized Isernia, a key German position on the way to Rome. These advances gave everybody hope that the war would soon be over, even though the Germans still occupied northern Italy and would not be easily budged.

By February 1944 talk of the invasion of Europe by the Allies was in the air. There was speculation as to what would happen if the Allies landed in the Netherlands first. Would the Germans open the dykes to flood the country in order to defend it as they'd said they would? Anne noted on a map that large portions of Amsterdam would disappear under water, and the occupants of the annexe entertained themselves with suggestions of what they would do if this happened.

▶ *Benito Mussolini, the Italian dictator (on the left) with Adolf Hitler. Mussolini's downfall was welcomed by the inhabitants of the annexe.*

The final months

With every day that passed, the inhabitants of the annexe became more anxious. They continued to listen to radio broadcasts, following closely the progress of the Allies. Their friends in the office also kept them informed of the situation, at the same time endeavouring to keep their spirits up.

Anne and the others were worried about the increasing burden put on their helpers. On 26 May Anne's heartfelt entry in her diary revealed her state of mind: "One day we're laughing at the comical side of life in hiding, and the next day we're frightened, and the fear, tension and despair can be read on our faces … Let something happen soon, even an air raid. Nothing can be more crushing than this anxiety."

On 6 June 1944 – D-day – the Allies landed in Normandy, on the French coast, and were engaged in furious combat with German troops. The invasion of Europe was announced at 12 noon on that day in a BBC broadcast.

▶ *US troops wade ashore from a landing craft on D-day. The Allied invasion of Europe brought a sense of hope to the inhabitants of the Secret Annexe.*

"A huge commotion in the annexe!" Anne wrote in her diary. At last the hideaways could allow themselves to be cautiously optimistic about the liberation and an end to the war. Margot started to make plans to go back to school the following September.

Security slip-ups

In the months leading up to this, the hideaways had begun to relax their guard somewhat, almost without realizing it. They continued to go about their daily routine, observing the quiet times, but they were becoming more careless, perhaps forgetting not to flush the toilet during working hours or leaving belongings downstairs in the evening. On one occasion Mr van Pels left his briefcase and wallet in the office. When they were discovered the next day by one of the warehouse staff and shown to Kugler, he was forced to say that they were his. When Kugler returned van Pels' belongings, some money was missing from the wallet. All they could do was hope that whoever took it would be satisfied.

On 11 April 1944 the warehouse was broken into and, without thinking, Mr van Pels went down and shouted "police" to get rid of the burglars. A man and a woman shone a torch into the warehouse and Peter and Mr van Pels ran back upstairs as fast as they could. This incident shocked the occupants of the annexe more than any other. They were terrified that the burglars would alert the police and they would be discovered. So, for a day and two nights, over the Easter break, the hideaways hardly dared move. They sat whispering into the darkness and each time they heard a creak, someone would say "shh". They scrambled around, trying to find warm clothes and something to use as a toilet, but for the most part they stayed still. When they heard a rattling of the bookcase and saw a light right in front of it, they thought the end had come. But, as the increasingly tense hours went by, no more was heard. Like the others, Anne was terrified, but she showed great courage, comforting Mrs van Pels and trying to behave "like a soldier". Eventually, after they had risked phoning Mr Kleiman, Miep and Jan turned up and gradually everything returned to normal.

On another occasion Peter forgot to lock the outside door at night, something all the inhabitants of the annexe had been scrupulously careful about in the past. One evening he forgot to unbolt the door so that Kugler and the staff could enter in the morning. If it hadn't been for Kugler's quick thinking (he smashed one of the kitchen windows in the office), an employee would have climbed in one of the back windows! Much later, after the war, a man who had lived in one of the houses overlooking the back of 263 Prinsengracht as a boy, recalled that he and his friend had seen a girl at the window of one of the rooms at the back (the Secret Annexe). Later, when he saw a photograph of her, he realized this must have been Anne. He may have mentioned it to his parents in passing. At any rate, the hideaways were becoming less vigilant and several people probably knew or suspected they were there.

More security alerts

At the beginning of 1944 a succession of burglaries once again put fear into those hiding in the annexe. In February Mr van Pels disturbed an intruder when he went to do his evening rounds downstairs. He thought the burglar had run off into the night, but the following morning Peter found the front door open. It looked as if the intruder had let himself in with a key, hidden in the building while Mr van Pels was downstairs, probably watching him as he returned upstairs, and then let himself out. This was a very worrying development for the hideaways since it meant that someone almost certainly knew of their whereabouts and had a key to the building. From then on, they lived in fear, Anne noting in her diary: "Who can have our key? … If the thief is one of the warehousemen, then he now knows someone is in the house at night …"

Is the end in sight?

As the hot summer progressed, most of the talk in the annexe was of liberation. They hardly dared to hope, yet they couldn't stop themselves. At the same time those in hiding learned that there was a resurgence of anti-Semitism because many Dutch people believed that some captured Jews had denounced their protectors to the Nazis. With a remarkable degree of understanding for a girl of her age Anne wrote that people should be able to see the situation from both sides. She wondered how Christians would react if they or their families were being tortured. Would they eventually

give in? No doubt many would. "So why ask the impossible of the Jews?"

Anne celebrated her 15th birthday on 13 June and her gifts included "a lovely bunch of peonies from Peter". In July a glut of strawberries arrived in crates and "for two days there were nothing but strawberries, strawberries, strawberries …" This was followed by nine kilos of peas. On 21 July the inhabitants of the annexe heard of the assassination attempt on Hitler's life, this time by a general in the army. "Now at last things are really going well!" Anne told "Kitty".

Betrayal

Anne's last letter to her diary is dated Tuesday, 1 August 1944. Three days later, on the morning of Friday, 4 August, the German Security Service (SD) burst into the office at 263 Prinsengracht and told the workers to stay where they were. They marched into Kleiman's office and soon after, seeming to know what they were doing, went upstairs to the bookcase and opened the door to the Secret Annexe. They arrested everyone there,

◀ *By August 1944 Allied troops had fought their way inland. Here, British soldiers storm a German-occupied French farmhouse. Resistance was fierce.*

pausing only to let them collect a few belongings. When the Gestapo left with their prisoners, Bep, Miep and Jan went upstairs and rescued what they could.

The hideaways had almost certainly been betrayed, but it was never discovered by whom. The office staff had their suspicions – a warehouse worker called van Maaren had been stealing from the company and was said to have told a fellow worker "there are Jews hidden in the building", but he never confessed. One thing Kleiman and Kugler knew for certain was that some of the warehouse staff suspected or guessed there were people hiding at the back of the house. Van Maaren had even set traps, although when questioned by his employers he said this was to catch the burglar. No one could prove otherwise.

Aftermath

After their arrest, Anne and the other occupants of the Secret Annexe, along with Victor Kugler and Jo Kleiman, were taken to a holding cell in the Gestapo headquarters on Euterpestraata in South Amsterdam.

Miep Gies and Bep Voskuijl were allowed to remain at the office. It was thanks to Miep, who saved Anne's diaries, scattered papers and many of the family's photograph albums, that these precious belongings were preserved. When she went through the rooms of the annexe, after her friends had been taken away, she picked up what she could and without knowing why she took Anne's shawl from the back of the bathroom door. "Even though my arms were filled with papers, I reached out and grabbed the shawl with my fingers. I still don't know why." Later, Otto Frank gave the shawl to Miep to keep in memory of Anne.

◀ *Victor Kugler survived the war. He moved to Canada, where this photograph was taken in 1978.*

The arresting officer

Karl Silberbauer, an Austrian-born police officer, was in charge of the arrest of the people hiding in the Secret Annexe. He forced Victor Kugler to take him and his men upstairs and as they pulled back the secret door they drew their revolvers. Once inside, Silberbauer grabbed Otto's briefcase, scattering the contents (Anne's papers) all over the floor. The exposure of Silberbauer as the arresting officer was made by the Nazi-hunter Simon Wiesenthal in 1963. The newspapers quoted Silberbauer as saying that "the Frank family was just one of many Jewish families who were rounded up by the Gestapo".

Kugler and Kleiman were separated from the others and were taken away to another cell. Later, the man in charge of their arrest – Silberbauer – questioned the Franks, the van Pels and Pfeffer. He asked them if they knew of any other Jews in hiding in Amsterdam. When Otto said that he didn't, they were taken back to their cells for the night. The next day they were sent to a prison called the Huis van Bewaring on the Weteringschans. Here they were held for two days in dreadful conditions before being sent to Westerbork transit camp. Kugler and Kleiman were also interrogated, and later that evening they were taken to Amstelveensweg prison in Amsterdam. There they were questioned again about who owned the business on Prinsengracht and again Kugler insisted that he and Mr Kleiman owned the firm, not Otto Frank. This was the truth.

Westerbork

By this time, Westerbork transit camp had grown to be almost a town. It contained a hospital, a school, shops, a telephone exchange and even an old people's home. Beyond the fence was a farm, which was tended by the inmates of the camp. There was even a cabaret, a choir and a ballet troupe that gave performances. A railway line ran right into the middle of the camp. Every Tuesday morning trains would leave from here, taking large numbers of prisoners to the camps in the east.

Liberation begins too late

Brussels and Antwerp were liberated on 4 September 1944 and in the Netherlands a joyful hysteria was in the air. People thought that the liberation of their country was finally at hand. This became known as "Mad Tuesday" because the victorious Allied armies failed to show up and the occupying Germans became even more brutal in their desperation to hold on to their captured territory. Two days after this Kugler and Kleiman were taken from Amstelveensweg prison to Weteringschans, where the occupants of the annexe had been held on 6 and 7 August. On 11 September, they were sent to Amersfoort transit camp, where they did hard labour, punctuated by roll calls and beatings. Jo Kleiman suffered a gastric haemorrhage and was unable to continue working. On 18 September he was released due to illness.

Sent to almost certain death

The occupants of the annexe were transported from Westerbork to Auschwitz in Poland. They were on the last train to leave the Netherlands for the extermination camps on 3 September 1944. This deportation meant almost certain death for many who were crammed into the overcrowded cattle-cars. The last train from Westerbork contained 1,019 people. Each car was packed with about 75 people, who had only one small bucket of water for

drinking and one larger one for use as a toilet. The journey to the camp took three days, during which time no one could stretch out because of lack of space. Many prisoners were already suffering from dysentery and some of the weakest died on the way.

When they arrived at their destination the prisoners were herded into groups of males and females. These groups were then divided into two columns: those who could work and those who could not. The group of non-workers included the sick, the elderly and children under fifteen. These people were told that transport was waiting to take them to the camp. Each lorry had a red cross painted on its side. Those who were too weak to walk scrambled aboard, only to be driven to immediate execution in the gas chambers inside the camp. Anne had just turned 15 and so escaped this fate.

The prisoners left behind endured an hour-long march to the gates of Auschwitz, over which were written the words "Arbeit Macht Frei" ("Work Brings Freedom"). A huge factory complex near Auschwitz, operated by the IG Farben

▶ *An exhausted female prisoner stares blankly through the barbed wire at Auschwitz.*

company, used large numbers of the camp inmates as forced labour. No thought was given to the safety of the workers, so the death toll in the factory was extremely high. Sick or well, people were forced to take risks to increase production. In truth, the only "freedom" from work was death.

Otto Frank survives

The fate of all but one of the inhabitants of the annexe was to die in a concentration camp in Poland, Germany or Austria. Only Otto Frank survived and it was he who recalled the death of Herman van Pels on 6 September, 1944 in the Auschwitz gas chambers just before they were dismantled in November 1944. It is not known in which concentration camp Auguste van Pels died, but this occurred sometime in the spring of 1945. She had been moved from Auschwitz to Bergen-Belsen, then to Buchenwald. The last recorded sighting of her was on yet another journey, this time to the concentration camp at Theresienstadt in Czechoslovakia on 9 April 1945 and it is likely that she died there. The van Pels' only son, Peter, died on 5 May 1945 in Mauthausen camp in Austria, having

been forced to march there, sick and hungry, from Auschwitz. It was just three days before the Mauthausen camp was liberated by the Allies. Fritz Pfeffer died in the Neuengamme concentration camp in Germany on 20 December 1944, after he had been transferred there from either Buchenwald or Sachsenhausen.

Fate of Anne and Margot

Otto, Edith, Margot and Anne Frank were in the Auschwitz-Birkenau camp together, but male and female prisoners were kept in separate sections of the camp. Edith succumbed to hunger and exhaustion and died on 6 January, 1945. At the end of October 1944, Margot and Anne were transported to Bergen-Belsen, near Hanover, Germany. Here a typhoid epidemic raged in the winter of 1944–45, the result of appallingly unhygienic conditions, which got worse as the camp's population swelled.

The disease killed thousands of prisoners, including Margot and, a little later, Anne. Anne died in late February or early March 1945, just weeks before

▶ *Conditions at Bergen-Belsen, where Anne and Margot died, were horrific. This photograph was taken shortly after the camp was liberated.*

Numbers of Jews killed, by country

- Germany   160,000
- Netherlands   106,000
- Czechoslovakia   277,000
- Hungary   305,000
- Poland   3,000,000
- Austria   65,000
- Romania   365,000
- France   83,000
- Lithuania   135,000
- Latvia   80,000
- Belgium   24,000
- USSR   1,000,000

British troops liberated the camp on 12 April 1945.

Jo Kleiman lived the rest of his life in Amsterdam, where he died in 1959. Victor Kugler managed to escape from his work group on 28 March 1945. He emigrated to Canada in 1955 and died in Toronto in 1981. Miep and Jan Gies stayed in Amsterdam and had a family. They stayed in touch with Otto Frank, who was reunited with them after the war. Bep Voskuijl died in Amsterdam in 1983 after a happy marriage and the children she had always wanted.

Otto Frank survived the camps. When Auschwitz was liberated by Russian troops on 27 January 1945, he was repatriated and returned to Holland via Odessa, a Russian port on the Black Sea, and Marseilles in the South of France. On 3 June 1945 Otto arrived back in Amsterdam and left no stone unturned in his quest to find out what had happened to his wife and daughters. He continued to live in the city until 1953 when he moved to Basel, in Switzerland, to be with his sister and family. That same year Otto remarried. His second wife was Elfriede (Fritzi) Markovits Geiringer, a Jewish woman who had also survived Auschwitz. Until his death in 1980, aged 91, Otto continued to share Anne's true story with the world.

◀ *British troops round up camp guards at Bergen-Belsen on the day of liberation, 12 April 1945.*

The diary:

A memorial to Anne

When Miep Gies picked up the scattered pages of Anne's diary and locked them in a drawer downstairs for safekeeping, it was an instinctive and protective action.

She couldn't have realized how important the diary would become, that millions of people would read the published version. Miep had not read Anne's diary, but she had no intention of letting the young girl's precious thoughts get into the wrong hands. She kept the diary, unread, hoping that one day she would be able to return it to Anne. After the war, she gave it to Otto, Anne's father, the only survivor of the Secret Annexe. Today, the diary can be seen in the Anne Frank Museum, which was established by Otto Frank at 263 Prinsengracht in Amsterdam.

A record for posterity

Although at first Anne had written the diary for herself, the chance hearing of a radio broadcast encouraged her to write a record for posterity. In 1944 she heard Gerrit Bolkestein of the Dutch government-in-exile on the radio. In his broadcast he said that after the war he would collect and publish eyewitness accounts of the Dutch people under the German occupation. This gave Anne, whose dream was to be a journalist, an added incentive for writing her diary. As well as acting as her confidante, it would be her first-hand account of a life in hiding during the occupation. In fact, she kept two versions: one was deeply personal; the other was written with a view to publication.

In Anne's memory

After the war Otto Frank decided to honour his daughter's memory – and grant her wish – by publishing the diary.

▶ *Otto Frank, a photograph taken before his death in 1980.*

◀ *The statue of Anne Frank which stands today in Amsterdam.*

The first edition, in 1947, was published in Dutch under the simple title *The Diary of a Young Girl*. The first print run was only a modest 1,500 copies. In his original edit, Otto selected passages from Anne's original unedited and amended versions. He took the decision to leave out several passages relating to Anne's sexuality, as well as some particularly hurtful comments she had made about her mother and others.

After Otto's death

When Otto died, at the age of 91, he left his daughter's papers to the Netherlands State Institute for War Documentation in Amsterdam. Since first publication, the authenticity of the diary had been in doubt (or at least thought by some to be a fake), so the Institute decided they must investigate and prove its authenticity once and for all. The *Critical Edition*, published in 1986, was the result of this investigation, which showed that the diary was the genuine article. In the *Critical Edition*, Anne's original unedited diary is referred to as "a", her second edited version is "b" and her father's

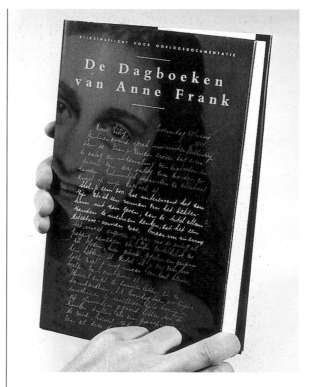

▲ The *Critical Edition of Anne's Diary, which was published in the Netherlands in Dutch.*

version (*The Diary of a Young Girl*) is "c". In the "b" version she used pseudonyms for most of the people mentioned, including herself. The van Pels were called the van Daans and Fritz Pfeffer was referred to as Albert Dussel. When Otto Frank came to edit the manuscript he respected Anne's wishes with regard to all but his family and helpers, who are referred to by their real names in the published versions.

A moving testament

Anne's diary is not only a testament to her lost youth but also the most poignant eyewitness account ever written of the Holocaust period. Anne's gift is in her words; through them she allows us to know her, her hopes and fears, and the secrets of her heart. Reading her diary, we experience with her the joys and setbacks of adolescence, the frustration and fear of a life in hiding, and the optimism that shines through in spite of everything: "If God lets me live, I'll go out into the world and work for mankind! I now know that courage and happiness are needed first!"

◀ *The* Critical Edition *was launched in Amsterdam in 1986. The publication of this edition of the diary was undertaken to silence once and for all people who thought that Anne's diary was faked. Here, the compilers explain their editorial methods – and the scientific examinations used – to the press.*

Glossary

Allegiance Loyalty to a government or monarch.

Annexe Extra, separate accommodation within a building.

Anti-Semitism Hostility towards Jews.

Arbitrary Decision made at random, usually by an oppressor.

Aryan Shared language of a group of people. A term improperly used in Nazi Germany to mean non-Jewish German.

Authentic Reliable, genuine.

Black market Place for illegally buying goods in short supply.

Blitzkrieg Aggressive military campaign intended to bring about quick victory.

Capitulate Surrender under certain conditions.

Collaborator Traitor who co-operates with the enemy.

Communism System of society in which everyone works for the common good.

Concentration camp Place where political prisoners or "enemy aliens" are detained.

Confidante Trusted person.

Constellation Group of fixed stars.

Counterpart Corresponding person or thing.

Decree Order or judgement decided by authority.

Democracy Government by the people, favouring social equality.

Denounce Inform against or publicly accuse someone.

Dyke Natural ditch or dam, especially those by the sea in Holland.

Edit Prepare for publication.

Elite Select group or class, considered to be the best.

Epidemic A widespread disease that affects a community at a particular time.

Expeditionary Fleet or men sent in for specific purpose, to do the job quickly.

Fascism Extreme right-wing or authoritarian views.

Fugitive Someone who is fleeing from danger.

Gas chamber A building used to kill prisoners by gas poisoning.

Genetically unfit Not of suitable origin, having "unsuitable" hereditary genes.

Gestapo Nazi secret police.

Great Depression The collapse of the world economy in 1929.

Holocaust Large-scale destruction, especially by fire.

Liberate Set free. The Liberation was the freeing of countries from German occupation during World War Two.

Memoir Personal account of events, written from memory.

Neutrality Exclusion from the hostilities of other countries; a neutral country is exempted from taking part in a war.

Paramilitary A military group that is organized in a similar way to the main military force, but is sub-ordinate to them (*from Greek para meaning "beside"*).

Paratroopers Parachute troops.

Posterity Future generations.

Prohibition An order that forbids something.

Propaganda Organized scheme to put forward political beliefs.

Pseudonym Made-up name.

Purge Elimination of people regarded as undesirable.

Qualm Uneasy feeling or doubt about a situation.

Ratify Formally accept or confirm agreement in writing.

Repatriate To return someone to the country in which they first lived.

Resistance Secret organization that resists foreign authority in a conquered country.

Resurgence Something that re-emerges or rises again.

Ruse Trick or device for deceiving the enemy.

Sabotage Deliberate destruction of enemy plans or equipment by covert (secret) means.

Sanctuary Place of refuge for fugitives from law.

Scapegoat Person getting the blame that should fall on others.

Segregate Separate or set apart.

Self-righteous Being right or virtuous in one's own eyes.

Skirmish Sudden outbreak of fighting.

Slump Sudden fall (*in prices*).

Sterilization Depriving a living being of the power to reproduce by removing reproductive organs.

Succumb To give in to force.

Suppress Use force to restrain something.

Swastika Originally an ancient good luck symbol, depicting arms in a clockwise cross, it was used by the Nazis on their flag.

Synagogue Jewish place of worship.

Testament Written statement of beliefs.

Transit camp Place for the temporary accommodation of soldiers or refugees.

Underground press Publications produced in secret.

Timeline

1889 12 May Otto Frank is born in Frankfurt am Main, Germany.

1900 16 January Edith Holländer is born in Aachen, Germany.

1909 Otto returns to Germany from New York on the death of his father.

1914-1918 Frank brothers serve in German army during World War One.

1925 May 12 Otto and Edith marry.

1926 February 26 Margot Frank is born in Frankfurt am Main.

1929 12 June Anne Frank is born in Frankfurt am Main.

1931 March Frank family moves to 24 Ganhoferstrasse in the Poets' Corner of Frankfurt.

1933 January Hitler becomes Chancellor of Germany; **Summer** Otto makes plans to move to the Netherlands; **Autumn** Otto becomes manager of the Opekta-Works in Amsterdam; **5 December** Edith and Margot join Otto in Amsterdam.

1934 February Anne moves to Amsterdam and begins at the Montessori nursery.

1937 The van Pels leave Osnabruck, Germany and flee to the Netherlands.

1938 Fritz Pfeffer leaves Germany for the Netherlands; **9-10 November** Kristallnacht.

1939 Anne's maternal grandmother joins the family in Amsterdam.

1940 1 December the Opekta-Works moves to 263 Prinsengracht; **8 May** Otto transfers the ownership of his business to Victor Kugler and Johannes Kleiman, renaming it Trading Company Gies & Co.; **Summer** Margot and Anne attend the Jewish Lyceum in Amsterdam.

1942 January Granny Holländer dies; **12 June** Anne's 13th birthday; she is given the diary.

1942 5 July Margot gets "call-up" papers; **6 July** Frank family go into hiding in the Secret Annexe; **13 July** The van Pels arrive at the Secret Annexe; **16 November** Fritz Pfeffer moves in to share Anne's room.

1944 4 August The occupants of the Secret Annexe are discovered; **8 August** After being interrogated, those from the Secret Annexe are transported to Westerbork camp; **3 September** The prisoners are sent to Auschwitz concentration camp in Poland on the last train. A week after their arrival there, Herman van Pels dies; **October** Anne and Margot are sent to Bergen-Belsen; **20 December** Fritz Pfeffer dies in Neuengamme concentration camp.

1945 6 January Edith Frank dies in Auschwitz; **27 January** Otto Frank is freed when Auschwitz is liberated by the Russian Army; **March** Margot and Anne die of typhus in Bergen-Belsen, a few weeks before the camp is liberated by the British Army; **Spring** Auguste van Pels dies in Theresienstadt concentration camp; **5 May** Peter van Pels dies in Mauthausen concentration camp in Austria; **3 June** Otto Frank returns to Amsterdam.

1947 The diary of Anne Frank is published in Dutch.

1986 The *Critical Edition* of Anne's diary is published.

Further reading

Anne Frank House, (2001), *The World of Anne Frank*, London: Macmillan

Davidowitz, Lucy S, (1987), *The War Against the Jews*, London: Penguin

The Diary of Anne Frank, Critical Edition, (1989), New York and London: Doubleday/Viking

Frank, Otto H. and Pressler, Mirjam, translated by Susan Massotty, (1995), *Anne Frank: the Diary of a Young Girl*, New York: Doubleday; (1997), London: Penguin

Gies, Miep with Gold, Alison Leslie, (1987), *Anne Frank Remembered*, New York: Bantam Press

Gold, Alison Leslie, (1997), *Memories of Anne Frank: Reflections of a Childhood Friend*, New York: Scholastic Press

Lee, Carol Ann, (1999), *Roses from the Earth: the biography of Anne Frank*, London and New York: Viking Penguin

Lindwer, Willy, (1991), *The Last Seven Months of Anne Frank*, New York: Pantheon

Moore, Bob, (1997), *Victims and Survivors: The Nazi Persecution of the Jews in the Netherlands 1940-45*, New York: St Martin's Press

Muller, Melissa, (1999), *Anne Frank: the biography*, London: Bloomsbury

Tames, Richard, (1998), *Anne Frank*, Oxford: Heinemann

van der Rol, Rund and Verhoeven, Rian, (1993), *Anne Frank: Beyond the Diary*, New York and London: Penguin Group

Chronicle of the 20th Century, (1988), London: Chronicle Longman

Index